After Legalization

Understanding the Future of Marijuana Policy

Jon Walker

FDL Writers Foundation
5731 Potomac Ave. NW
Washington DC 20016

Bring the author to your live event: AfterLegalization@gmail.com

Cover design by David Cran
Formatting by Polgarus Studio

Printed in the United States of America

Library of Congress Control Number: 2013958045

ISBN 978-0-9912397-1-9
ISBN 978-0-9912397-0-2 (ebook)

Thanks to all the people who helped make this possible over the past two years.

I want to specifically thank Brian Sonenstein, Zach Tomanelli, Jane Hamsher, Molly Gordon, David Cran, and Nathan Rostron. I want to thank John Desmond Dolan and Minnesota NORML for their financial support. I also want to extend special thanks to my girlfriend, Stephanie Condon. She was an invaluable help, spending many late nights working with me to craft this book. I can't thank her enough for all she did for me.

Table of Contents

Introduction - The End of Prohibition

There's no longer a question of whether marijuana will be legalized in the United States, only a question of when and how. The historic 2012 passage of marijuana legalization ballot initiatives in Colorado and Washington State made that clear.

The idea may seem unbelievable to those who grew up during the War on Drugs, and who were subjected to countless government-funded anti-pot public service announcements. The simple fact is that marijuana legalization has become increasingly inevitable. It may not happen immediately or all at once, but legal and social trends are heading in that direction.

Once we accept that legalization is inevitable, the important question becomes *how* marijuana is legalized. For each of the wide variety of legal consumer goods, the federal government has a distinct approach. Apples are legal, and they can be sold to anyone and grown by almost anyone. Distilled alcohol is legal, but only those over 21 can buy it, only specially licensed stores can sell it, and only licensed distillers can produce it. Similarly, handguns are legal but are often subject to many restrictions, including background checks and permit requirements. Morphine is legal, but only in specific medical settings under a doctor's supervision; outside of that, its use and sale is a serious crime.

While I am an advocate and activist for legalization, this book is not my utopian vision of how marijuana legalization should proceed. The future depicted in these pages is not exactly the one I want, nor are the regulatory and legal systems described necessarily the ones I think would work best. This is not my perfect world, nor simply a how-to guide for regulating cannabis. Rather, this look forward is based on historical examples, current trends, past legislation, and my experience as a political strategist. The fact is, politics and regulation are often very messy. They are driven by painful compromises, ideological arguments, greed, and sometimes good old-fashioned stupidity. If people really want to shape policy, they need to understand the forces at play. I've tried my best to leave my personal bias at the door and instead take an objective look at existing data and information—relating to marijuana and other products—to construct the most likely outcome.

As the public makes up its collective mind about whether or not marijuana should be legal, it is important to start considering the next big step: How exactly will we, as a country, treat and regulate marijuana? By laying out what I think is the most likely outcome, I want to get people thinking about the dozens of questions, big and small, that will emerge once marijuana moves from the black market to the legal market, to prepare them for the many smaller political fights that lie ahead.

I want people to think about the extent to which the government should regulate marijuana and what our attitudes toward it as a society should be.

The inevitability of marijuana legalization is clear from the polling and demographic data. In 1995, Gallup found that only 25 percent of Americans thought marijuana should be legal, while 73 percent thought it should remain illegal. But from the mid-'90s onward, support for marijuana legalization has grown steadily and significantly. By 2013, there had been a sea change in public opinion. That was the first year Gallup found a majority of the public, 58 percent, thought marijuana should be legal, while only 39 percent thought it should remain illegal.[1]

The dramatic shift in the politics surrounding marijuana use over the past three decades can be illustrated with the stories of three individuals. Back in 1987, during the height of Ronald Reagan's anti-drug campaign, the president nominated Douglas Howard Ginsburg for the Supreme Court. However, once it was revealed Ginsburg had used marijuana several years earlier, it created such a political firestorm that he withdrew his name from consideration. By 1992, Bill Clinton admitted to trying marijuana after being asked a direct question about it on the presidential campaign, but he did his best to downplay his experimentation by famously saying, "I experimented with marijuana a time or two, and didn't like it. I didn't inhale and I didn't try it again."[2] It was such a ridiculous answer that it quickly became a punch line, yet it sent the right political message. Clinton wanted voters to know he thought it was mistake—one they should avoid themselves. It was an embarrassing character flaw, but not a devastating one. A mere 16 years later, when Barack Obama ran for president, the fact that he had very publicly written and talked about his frequent past use of marijuana was a political non-issue. If anything, some saw it as a political plus, because it demonstrated his honesty and helped Obama relate to the young voters who drove his victory. Obama's response to the same question asked of Clinton was that he "inhaled frequently; that was the point."

Now picture how much this story will change in the next three decades. Public opinion isn't just shifting, but shifting exponentially. In the ten years between 1995 and 2005, support for legalization grew by 11 points nationwide, from 25 to 36 percent. It grew by another 10 points in the five years between 2005 and 2010. And after the historic victories in Colorado and Washington, support jumped to 58 percent. When the issue of marijuana legalization first appeared on the ballot in Colorado in 2006, it was roundly rejected with 41 percent voting in favor and 59 percent against it. Just six years later, public opinion had completely flipped. In 2012, Colorado became the first state to legalize marijuana when 55 percent of voters supported Amendment 64.

To understand why this trend is destined to continue, one should start by looking at the demographics. Opinions about marijuana heavily break down by age. In 2011, 62 percent of adults under 30 thought marijuana should be legal, while only 31 percent of senior citizens felt the same way. A new generation in support of reform is taking over. Every year, young pro-marijuana adults are reaching voting age, while older opponents of reform are, to put it bluntly, dying out. At the same time, one-time opponents are changing their minds on the issue. In the not-too-distant future, there will be a supermajority of people who support marijuana legalization. And when that happens, the federal prohibition of marijuana will end soon after.

This book is written from the perspective of someone in the year 2030 describing what America looks like after federal marijuana legalization has been in place for a few years. It is intended to answer the two big "how" questions: how marijuana will be treated as a legal product, and how this change will come about. I will show in a very tangible way what legalization will mean for regular people and give a detailed explanation for why things may turn out that way.

It is easy to scare people with the unknown. Even if we understand that legalization is inevitable, it can still be difficult to envision what legal marijuana will look like. One goal of this book is to demystify marijuana by providing the most realistic vision of how marijuana legalization will likely function in America.

Back at the beginning of the 20th century when extremely few Americans had tried marijuana, prohibitionists like Harry Anslinger, the commissioner of the Federal Bureau of Narcotics, could get away with making ridiculous claims. He told the American people marijuana use could turn the youth into crazed murderers who would lose their minds forever. He linked marijuana use to every terrifying thing he could think of: insanity, violence, the deflowering of white women, and even Communist plots. Anslinger began his article "Marijuana – Assassin of Youth" in The American Magazine by claiming, "Not long ago the body of a young girl lay crushed on the sidewalk after a plunge from a Chicago apartment window. Everyone called it suicide, but actually it was murder. The killer was a narcotic known to America as marijuana, and to history as hashish. Used in the form of cigarettes, it is comparatively new to the United States and as a coiled rattlesnake. How many murders, suicides, robberies and maniacal deeds it causes each year, especially among the young, can only be conjectured. In numerous communities it thrives almost unmolested, largely because of official ignorance of its effects."[3]

By the beginning of the 21st century, so many American adults had at least tried marijuana that such absurd and unfounded scare tactics were no longer effective. Instead, opponents of legalization shifted their focus to the public's uncertainty about how legalization would work and natural aversion to change. Many attacks against Proposition 19, California's marijuana legalization initiative in 2010 that narrowly failed, focused not on the dangers of marijuana but on making voters worry about how it would be implemented. Los Angeles County Sheriff Lee Baca, who co-chaired the campaign against Proposition 19, attacked it as creating "a patchwork of thousands of conflicting local laws," which would end up a "jumbled legal mess."[4] Several prominent California newspapers reiterated this theme. For example, the LA Times editorial board warned voters Prop 19 would be an "invitation to chaos," because it would conflict with federal law and "would permit each of California's 478 cities and 58 counties to create local regulations regarding the cultivation, possession and distribution of marijuana. In other words, the law could change hundreds of times from county to county."[5] Often ignored in this patchwork argument against marijuana was the fact that almost everything in America, from alcohol to parking to septic tank installation, is treated in this "patchwork" manner. Local regulation is a natural and often necessary part of American governance. It frequently doesn't make sense to apply the same rules to urban environments as rural ones.

By showing in very concrete terms how legal marijuana would probably be handled and how it would impact the country in both good and bad ways, I hope to make it real to people, and to allay fears that arise from uncertainty. Marijuana legalization should not be a scary unknown but a clear policy choice. Ideally after reading this book, a citizen should have a clear idea of how—or, more accurately, how little—legalizing marijuana will change their lives and community. Those changes will be much less drastic than legalization's opponents would have us think. Numerous data points support this hypothesis, including the adoption of medical marijuana in certain states and the end of alcohol prohibition. There is also a wealth of data to draw from internationally, such as the several-decades-long de facto legal status of marijuana in the Netherlands.

An even more critical goal of this book is to start a conversation about what the next step should be for marijuana reform. In the past decade, much of the debate has focused on whether the plant is safe or harmful, whether prohibition does more good or more harm to society as a whole, and whether it should be legal or illegal. I'd like to move the conversation forward.

The best time to have this conversation is before a system is put in place. Once inertia takes over, big change becomes nearly impossible. The most powerful force in American politics isn't grassroots activism, party loyalty, or even money—it is inertia. For example, most Americans think the Electoral College is an unfair and idiotic way to choose the president, but inertia keeps this unpopular system in place. Once a framework is established, it creates an entire financial ecosystem of people, politicians, and businesses that entrench themselves within it. Even in the face of significant and overwhelming problems with the status quo, dismantling an existing system to create a better one requires tremendous focus and patience. If readers are unhappy with my predictions, let that motivate them to become advocates for putting a different system in place before the cement hardens.

This book takes place about 20 years from now, and many of the laws, policies, agencies, and people featured in it are fictional. Everything within these pages with a date that precedes 2014 actually happened. Of course, everything that takes place in the book's "present day" or after the year 2013 are my inventions. These predictions are drawn from comparisons with the end of alcohol prohibition and states' experiences with medical marijuana. The regulations recently adopted by Colorado and Washington State for their new, legalized recreational marijuana industry, as well as the federal government's treatment of tobacco and alcohol, provide a solid foundation for my analysis. I will repeatedly make reference to these real facts and real events—with plenty of citations—to make the case for why I think marijuana will be treated in the way it is in this book.

Of course, no one can predict the future with complete accuracy. However, if I can merely help move the national conversation from whether marijuana should be legalized to how it should be legalized, I will consider my book a success.

Chapter 1 - Where to Buy

It is 2030, you're at least 21 years of age, and you want to acquire some marijuana. If you live in part of the vast majority of the country that is "green," meaning it allows marijuana to be sold, you simply head to your nearest marijuana retailer. It is likely to be a small, nondescript store with very minimal advertising on the exterior—the type of place you would miss if you weren't looking for it.

Marijuana stores run the gamut, but here are three examples. In some parts of the country, your only options are generic, government-run shops with a very sterile feel—for example, a government-controlled marijuana store in Durham, North Carolina, that goes by the exciting designation of Durham County Cannabis Control Commission Store location Apex Highway. It was built in 2024. The location's name distinguishes it from the nearly identical Durham County Cannabis Control Commission Store location North Roxboro

RD. They are both technically run by the local county Alcohol Control Board under the guidance of the state government, which has a monopoly on cannabis sales.

Not all stores, however, are run by the government. Most marijuana stores tend to be rather tiny licensed neighborhood stores with only a modest selection, like one "mom-and-pop" shop operating out of a strip mall in Bridgewater, New Jersey. It is owned and operated by two brothers, Tom and Richard Stevenson, who named it T&R Marijuana for obvious reasons. They are good businessmen, but not the most creative. They started this business in 2023, right after the state legalized marijuana.

In some large metropolitan areas, it is possible to find numerous specialty shops that cater to high-end consumers and people into unusual varieties, or stores that specialize in strains bred for medical uses. The flagship store for Indica Aficionado, located in the heart of the "Oaksterdam district" in Oakland, is one such successful niche retailer that focuses on high-end buds. It is a small luxury chain with five locations throughout California. The first Indica Aficionado opened in 2017 in Santa Monica to target the true connoisseur in the newly legalized market. Because of its success as a niche retailer, the company expanded by building this large flagship store two years later. It chose Oakland because, as part of a tourism and downtown revitalization campaign in 2018, the city changed several zoning rules to officially create a pro-pot "Oaksterdam district." The store features much higher prices, but they are justified with unmatched selection, quality, and customer service. These three businesses capture the significant diversity in the industry across the country and will be highlighted throughout the book.

Jon Walker

Because New Jersey is a "green" state that has privately licensed stores and moderately tough regulations, T&R Cannabis provides one of the most remarkably average marijuana shopping experiences you can find. If you want to buy marijuana in Bridgewater, you head to the strip mall and find the small store with a sign that reads "T&R Cannabis" and contains the obligatory outline of a pot leaf. This out-of-the-way strip mall location happens to be one of the few commercial spaces in the area that is at least 1000 feet from any schools and playgrounds. T&R Cannabis is the only store in the strip mall that actually benefits from its otherwise poor location. When Washington State became one of the first two states to legalize marijuana retail, they adopted this regulation, creating a standard many states later adopted.

The T&R storefront is boring by law. New Jersey is one of many states that highly restrict displays of cannabis products and advertising. The window is frosted to prevent minors from seeing inside. The window's only decorations are the store's logo, the statement that it is a licensed marijuana retailer, a no-smoking sign, the lit up OPEN sign, and the mandatory 12"-by-12" sign composed of letters not less than half an inch in height, which states, "Restricted Access Area – No One Under 21 Years of Age Allowed."[1] The lack of storefront advertising is not much of a problem because T&R Cannabis doesn't need to worry about local competition: No other marijuana store may

---

[1] This is the exact restriction Colorado adopted in 2013 for its marijuana retailers.
Permanent Rules Related to the Colorado Retail Marijuana Code.
Colorado Department of Revenue. Sep 9, 2013
http://www.colorado.gov/cs/Satellite/Rev-MMJ/CBON/1251592984795

be within 1,000 feet of them. This is good news for the uncreative Stevenson brothers, whose pot-leaf sign gets the point across but is kind of lame.

The first thing you will notice when you try to walk into T&R Cannabis is that you can't. You can only walk into a small foyer and then must show your ID proving you are of age before being buzzed into the main store. People in the industry jokingly refer to this as the "check box." The double-door system is for checking ID, security, and to contain the often pungent smell of so much weed. Local fines or lawsuits from neighboring businesses against the rich aroma coming from marijuana retailers are not unheard of. For example, in 2012, the city of Denver, Colorado, received 288 odor complaints, of which 11 were related to marijuana. Many businesses as a result are required to install powerful air filter systems.[6] No one under 21 is even allowed in a marijuana store in most states, and it is one of the most strictly enforced regulations. This not only prevents underage people from buying marijuana, but it also makes it difficult for them to attempt to shoplift it.

The inside, however, is nothing like the drab exterior required by law. The small store is welcoming, colorful, and smells overwhelmingly of dank weed. The space not taken up with marijuana products is filled with enticing promotional posters, bright signs indicating specials, and vintage posters meant to give the place a '60s vibe—a cliché, but a remarkably common one in these stores.

Like most marijuana stores across the country, T&R Cannabis has a decent selection of marijuana-infused products, and different strains of marijuana herb to choose from. At this Jersey store you can buy up to the equivalent of six ounces.

Almost every green state sets a purchase limit from an ounce to a few pounds. Almost no one buys that much in a single trip, though; most people tend to buy only several grams at a time. Even heavy users of marijuana will likely consume no more than a few grams in a given day.

In large stretches of the country, buying marijuana is, for the most part, only slightly more difficult than buying a bottle of vodka. The regulatory nature of the marijuana system is very similar to that of hard alcohol, and like alcohol, the regulations governing marijuana are highly localized.

The country is divided into so-called "green" states and counties that allow for the sale of marijuana and the "straight" states and counties that prohibit its sale within their borders. Cannabis enthusiasts will sometimes derisively refer to states that don't allow the sale of marijuana as "square" states, a dual reference to old hippie slang for conservatives and the fact that many of these states are, in fact, fairly rectangular in shape.

When Congress passed the Regulation and Control of Cannabis Act of 2022, it closely followed the model established by the repeal of the 21st Amendment ending the prohibition of alcohol: The act only ended federal marijuana prohibition while allowing states to decide its legal status within their borders. The federal government supports local laws and helps keep marijuana from being transported to states that still prohibit it. Immediately after the 21st Amendment was ratified, roughly a third of states maintained their laws prohibiting alcohol. It wasn't until 1966, more than three decades later, that Mississippi finally became the last state to repeal its anti-alcohol laws. The same piecemeal initial buy-in occurred with marijuana.

Straight States

Seven states—Utah, Mississippi, Oklahoma, Wyoming, Idaho, Alabama, and Nebraska[II]—decided to keep the commercial growth and sale of marijuana illegal within their borders. But even these conservative states were not immune to the general push to liberalize marijuana laws. They significantly reduced their penalties for marijuana possession compared to the previous century, making personal marijuana use legal or, at most, technically just a civil infraction punishable by a small fine. It seems every year another state moves to full legalization.

Of the seven "straight" states, Wyoming and Idaho are unique cases. Two years before Congress passed the Regulation and Control of Cannabis Act (RCCA), Idaho pursued a path between legalization and prohibition, which thanks to legislative inertia, remains in place. Wyoming later copied the Idaho model. While the commercial sale and production of marijuana is prohibited in these states, it is legal for adults to grow and possess limited amounts of marijuana for their own personal use. This grow-your-own right was eventually expanded to allow residents to cooperatively grow marijuana as dues-paying members of non-profit marijuana co-ops. For residents of these states who want to acquire marijuana without driving to a neighboring green state, finding a co-op to join is not too difficult. Whether or not to replace the co-op system with full

---

[II] Conservatives tend to be the group most opposed to marijuana legalization. All seven of these states are in Gallup's list of the ten most conservative states.

legalization has been a perennial issue of debate in the legislatures of both states since the RCCA passed.

As a result of a series of court decisions, a version of this co-op model emerged in Spain in 2002. Possession of marijuana for personal use was not a crime in Spain, but it was illegal to use it in public, sell it, or traffic in it. This created a legal gray area that was eventually filled by cannabis social clubs, non-profit private cultivation clubs that provided members with access to marijuana. By 2010, over a hundred non-profit, member-based cannabis social clubs existed in the country.[7]

In the U. S., the vast majority of states allow the commercial growth and retail sale of marijuana within a regulated market, but 35 of 43 green states have adopted local option rules. Local option rules give counties and/or towns the ability to decide whether or not to allow marijuana retail locations, farmers, processing plants, and/or smoking lounges. Some municipalities ban all marijuana businesses, but others only ban certain types. That is why it is possible to end up with a truly bizarre situation similar to the one in Moore County, Tennessee. Moore is home to America's most popular whiskey distillery, Jack Daniels, but even in 2013 it was still a "dry" county when it came to the retail sale of alcohol. It is legal for the company to make massive quantities of whiskey but illegal for regular people to buy basically any in the county.[8] In 2012 there was a tiny step toward reform. That year the distillery could finally start giving people only three small samples if they paid for a tour. Within states with local option rules, just under half of all localities at least initially banned marijuana retail stores and/or coffee shops.

While this obstacle can be inconvenient, most people find it only mildly burdensome. As a rule, the more localities in a given area that ban marijuana retailers, the more valuable it becomes for at least one nearby town/county to allow them. In much of the country, one is rarely more than an hour's drive from at least one marijuana retailer. Most marijuana users who live in "straight" localities are often not even aware that their municipality has adopted such a rule. While marijuana retailers are banned in South Broad Brook, New Jersey, it is just a few miles to T&R Marijuana in Bridgewater. Most people just assume the placement of the stores results from happenstance or economic considerations rather than local ordinances.

Local option rules have a long history in the United States. They became popular in the 19th century when the temperance movement attempted to use them to spread prohibition gradually. Originally, the idea was to ban alcohol one county at a time before the movement became more ambitious. Local option rules remained popular as a compromise position following the end of prohibition, when roughly two-thirds of states adopted them. While the number of dry counties began to decrease starting in the 1930s, even in 2010 roughly 8 percent of the United States was still dry thanks to local option rules. Just under half of Mississippi still prohibited the production, advertising, sale, distribution, and transportation of alcohol nearly 80 years after federal prohibition officially ended.[9]

Large stretches of Mississippi remained dry for so long for both cultural and legal reasons. Mississippi is one of only a handful of states where a county is dry by default unless the county actively decides to turn wet. This is different from how the local option rules work in most other states, where localities have to actively choose to prohibit the sale of alcohol. While this may seem like a small technical distinction, it tends to create a big practical difference due to the power of inertia.

Most municipalities that adopted local marijuana sales bans did so right after marijuana was legalized in their state, when local opposition to marijuana retailers was at its peak. For example, after Colorado voters approved a marijuana legalization initiative in 2012, most Colorado municipalities adopted bans or temporary moratoriums on marijuana stores before retail sales started.[10] In the beginning, marijuana stores were limited to only a few parts of the state, with Denver being the only large city to allow for retail locations. Even though support for marijuana has grown dramatically, some of these bans remain in place, in part because of legislative inertia, and in part because of the political fusion of anti-marijuana sentiment with the financial backing of nearby marijuana businesses. While it would marginally benefit the marijuana industry as a whole to have more retail locations, it would significantly hurt local marijuana retailers if they were forced to face new competition. These vested local businessmen are basically the only ones that pay attention to and get actively involved in politics regarding these rather boring local ordinance issues.

A segment of an industry funding the political fight against its own expansion to prevent competition is a common occurrence in politics. One significant example was the 2012 election fight over Question 7 in Maryland, the ballot measure that allowed the building of a new casino in Prince George's County. It was the most expensive campaign in the state's history, but the millions of dollars in opposition ads weren't funded by groups opposed to gambling on moral or public policy grounds. A company with a casino in nearby West Virginia spent over $42 million on ads trying to convince the voters in Maryland that building a casino was a bad idea. Their goal was to keep out competition, and their campaign almost succeeded. Voters in the state narrowly approved the measure allowing the new casino, 52 percent yes to 48 percent no.[11]

Control States

The "green" states can be further subdivided into "control states" and "license states." The control states are those in which the government has a monopoly on major aspects of the marijuana business, while in license states, the sector is run completely by highly regulated and licensed private businesses. Most states, having concluded that marijuana and hard alcohol should share similar regulation and tax requirements, decided to expand their state alcohol agencies to encompass marijuana.

This is why in 2023 New Hampshire and Virginia decided marijuana could be legally sold only in some of the state-run alcohol stores that also have a monopoly on the sale of liquor. These state-run liquor stores are frequently called ABC stores, because they are often governed by Alcohol Control Boards. They tend to be bland, utilitarian stores that only sell high alcohol content products. The idea is to have all government-controlled products for people over 21 in one store for efficiency. This concept was not particularly popular with the liquor industry, which thought it helped marijuana compete with their business, so they lobbied state by state to prevent the practice from becoming more widespread. These piety fights, with one company or industry trying to gain every advantage over another, drive a lot of the regulatory rule-writing that few voters pay attention to.

North Carolina, Pennsylvania, West Virginia, and Maryland also created a government monopoly on retail marijuana sales but decided to establish government-run stores where only marijuana and marijuana products can be sold.[III] These are modeled after the ABC stores but remain separate entities. These government marijuana stores are run by the states' Cannabis Control Commissions and are known as CCC stores because of their CCC signs.

Almost all CCC stores in the country feel like bland clones of Durham County Cannabis Control Commission Store location Apex Highway. If you have been to one, you can pretty confidently say you know all of them. Driving up, the store looks like a nondescript cube on the edge of town. The only advertising is a tall, boring white sign with three big forest green C's and "Cannabis Store" in small print underneath. It makes the Stevenson brothers' sign for T&R Cannabis look like a stroke of marketing genius by comparison.

The front door bears the CCC emblem, store hours, and a warning that it is a crime to enter if under 21. Upon entering, you will notice they also use the double-door system but take it a step further. In the check box you are required to have a swipeable government-issued ID and look directly into the

---

[III] North Carolina and Pennsylvania directly operate government-run liquor stores. Maryland is an unusual mixed state. A few counties in Maryland run their own liquor stores. West Virginia holds a monopoly on the wholesaling of liquor but doesn't run its own alcohol retail outlets. States where the government is already heavily involved in the alcohol business are most likely to do the same for legal marijuana.

security camera. The ID must match the system's facial recognition software before you can be allowed in. Preventing kids from buying marijuana is a serious mission for the county government.

The inside echoes the Spartan feel of the outside. The first three words that come to mind are boring, sterile, and functional. Products are neatly arranged on the shelves, but otherwise the walls are plain white without any advertisements, decoration, or personality. A guiding philosophy of the government monopoly on liquor or cannabis is to make the experience unexciting so it doesn't encourage overconsumption. I can confidently say the Durham CCC store succeeded.

The marijuana business in Vermont, Montana, and Delaware functions under the same quasi-government monopoly system used for the liquor industry in some states, sometimes called an agency system[IV]: The government has a monopoly on the sales but doesn't actually run any stores. Privately-owned stores are contracted by the government to sell cannabis on the state's behalf for a commission. As a result, the physical stores tend to resemble the private stores in the "license states," but prices across the entire state are set by the government.

Overall, in about a fourth of the green states, marijuana is held in some form of state monopoly, while in the other three-fourths, state agencies license and regulate private companies.

When alcohol prohibition ended, the control model was seen as a way to allow the legal sale of alcohol while keeping it tightly regulated and limited. While alcohol prohibition was

---

[IV] Vermont and Montana currently use this system for liquor sales.

considered a policy failure by most Americans, by the time the 21st Amendment was ratified, many still viewed alcohol use as dangerous and bad for society. Government monopolies over the retailing and/or wholesaling retail of alcohol were adopted in several parts of the United States and a few European countries, with the goal of restricting sales and removing the private profit motive to maximize liquor consumption. Roughly a third of states went the control route after ending alcohol prohibition. In 2012, there were still 18 control states where the government had some form of monopoly over alcohol, although over the years the level of government involvement in these states had relaxed in different ways. During most of the 20th century, Vermont and Montana owned all the liquor stores in the state but in the mid-'90s eliminated their government-run stores and switched to an agency system in which they contracted with private companies.[12]

The control system for marijuana was primarily, but not exclusively, adopted in states that were already using it for high-proof alcohol. There are only a few states that use a licensing system for liquor but a control system for marijuana or vice versa. The move was considered the simplest and most logical way of regulating a new substance that necessitated similar restrictions to those imposed on liquor. It also, of course, eliminated the need to create whole new agencies.

Among marijuana users in control states, the biggest complaints are that there aren't enough stores for the population and that store hours are limited. There tend to be significantly fewer CCC stores than ABC stores. Of course, those who want to discourage smoking consider those facts to be positives. Both of these viewpoints are still held and debated over when it comes to liquor control. When Republican Gov. Bob McDonnell tried to privatize Virginia's state-run liquor business in 2011, one of his big selling points was that it would replace the 332 ABC stores with 1,000 private retailers, making it much more convenient for regular people to buy liquor. Despite aggressive lobbying by the governor the idea was killed by the legislature, in large part because analysis determined that over the long term a private system would bring in less revenue for the state.[13]

In marijuana control states, there are occasional campaigns to privatize the system to different degrees. These efforts are backed by a combination of cannabis users, libertarian advocates, and industry groups. As with alcohol, the exact nature of what and how much direct government involvement should be in the market will continue to be a source of political debate for decades to come. While the level of government involvement in alcohol control states has loosened over the decades, the pace has been extremely slow. It wasn't until Washington State voters approved Initiative 1183 in 2011 that a control state moved to completely privatize all aspects of its liquor sales.[14] The fact that a year after privatization was implemented, consumers were actually paying roughly 7 percent more for the same bottle of liquor meant this initiative didn't exactly generate a wave of enthusiasm for similar reforms around the country.[15]

License States

The other main way to run a marijuana system is for the government to simply license and regulate private companies.

Both California and New Jersey are license states, for example, but with noticeably different regulations. Most states that use this model tend to give the responsibility to whatever agency already regulated alcohol. This is what Initiative 502 did in 2012, putting the Washington State Liquor Control Board in charge of regulating the new legalized recreational marijuana business.

A few states with large established medical marijuana systems that predated legalization naturally decided to use them as a basis for recreational marijuana. Yet these medical marijuana states significantly overhauled their systems when they embraced full legalization. This was often done to try to win over the vested stakeholders in the medical marijuana industry, who could become enemies of particular reform bills if they saw legalization as threatening their livelihood. This is part of what bedeviled California's Proposition 19 during the 2010 election. For decades, Humboldt Country had been famous for being pot-friendly and one of the most productive marijuana growing regions in the state, yet a greater percentage of the county voted against the initiative than the state did as a whole.[16]

Marijuana activists learned their lesson from their defeat in 2010. The 2012 Colorado legalization campaign did an effective job reaching out to the large medical marijuana industry and addressing their concerns. Amendment 64 in Colorado not only used the regulatory system for medical marijuana as the foundation for regulating legal marijuana, but it also gave pre-existing medical marijuana dispensaries special advantages. For example, these businesses qualify for special, significantly lower application fees for expanding their businesses into recreational sales compared to new companies entering the market.[17]

Legalization in California was heavily influenced by its long history with medical marijuana. The Golden State was not only the first state to set up a medical marijuana system, but it also had some of the most lax regulations and highly decentralized oversight. The ease with which Californians could obtain a medical recommendation meant the state had over a decade of experience with quasi-legalization before it officially allowed recreational use. This made voters more comfortable with commercial marijuana business and meant California was one of the only states with a large pre-existing industry in place to lobby against overly restrictive regulations when legalization was adopted. As a result, California has some of the least restrictive rules in the country, which makes easier to run a specialty business like Indica Aficionado.

If you take a stroll through the Oaksterdam district in Oakland, there is no doubt Indica Aficionado's flagship location is only one of many marijuana-related businesses. The popular district only exists because California is one of the few states that, after it approved legalization in 2016, technically allowed marijuana businesses to exist in close proximity, and Oakland was one of the few cities in the state that didn't adopt its own tough local restrictions. Large, colorful signs advertise Indica Aficionado's presence. Massive storefront windows let passersby see the diversity and quality of their offerings and let the rich smell spill out the open doors to entice customers to enter. This "freedom to smell" is one of the regulatory advantages that make the small Oaksterdam district so friendly to marijuana businesses and customers. It is also one of the only places people are explicitly allowed to smoke in public, although enforcing laws against public marijuana smoking is not a priority anywhere in the Bay Area. In the district you often see people enjoying marijuana in the outdoor seating sections of local businesses or in the small park at the center. There are almost always a few food trucks in the area. These mobile snack purveyors love the district for obvious reasons.

Part connoisseur mecca, showroom for producers, and passion project, Indica Aficionado is more than just a store. It is an experience, an advertisement for the chain, and a tourist destination in its own right. People don't just come here to buy marijuana. The store often hosts unveilings of new products, talks by local growers, and lectures from their cannabis sommeliers. The inside is spacious and a monument to the sophistication cannabis can achieve. The place has high ceilings and a modern architectural design. The actual decoration is minimal because every design element is focused on showcasing the hundreds of varieties of bud for sale. They consider their wares not just products but pieces of art.

While advertising and location rules are more relaxed than the rest of country, prohibiting people under 21 from entry is still strictly required. The single front door is normally open on nicer days but always guarded by a helpful but firm employee who checks IDs. Indica Aficionado tries to minimize this inconvenience by making the ID check part of a welcoming routine that also functions as a subtle sales pitch. You probably won't notice the three small, strategically placed cameras monitoring the entrance and ID check, the footage from which the store is required to keep for a month in case of random age audits.

In a license state, a private company that wants to sell marijuana needs to be licensed to do so by state and local governments. The licensing fees tend to run into the thousands, and licenses will be revoked if a retailer is caught breaking state law by, for instance, selling to minors or selling after hours. As with alcohol, every state has set retail sales hours, normally the same hours set for alcohol sales. For example, in Connecticut, retail marijuana can't be sold after 9 p.m.—the same hour the sales of hard liquor must stop.

In addition to these rules, private retailers must comply with all relevant local and state ordinances. Most towns ban marijuana retail within a set distance from schools, playgrounds, churches, and other locations where children are likely to congregate.

Chapter 2 – What to Buy: Brands, Selection, and Big Marijuana

Once you enter T&R Cannabis, you will notice the space is small but fully utilized. The store is divided into three main sections: The right wall is dedicated to cured buds, with some 40 different strains on display. As required by federal regulations, they are all free of enhancement, additives, and added flavoring. Keeping legal drugs out of the hands of minors is a driving force behind many regulations of both marijuana and tobacco. The Food and Drug Administration in 2009 outlawed the sale of candy or fruit-flavored cigarettes in an attempt to discourage tobacco use by youth, and the same basic regulation was applied to marijuana once it was legalized.[18]

Almost all the pure buds sold here and across the country are certified organic. This is not required by law, but rather how the market has evolved to meet consumer demand. Regulations require a "complete list of all nonorganic pesticides, fungicides, and herbicides used during the cultivation of the retail marijuana."[V] Even though a certain level of pesticides is considered safe by the government, many marijuana users don't find the idea of smoking chemicals appealing. The notice on a package can turn off enough consumers to make it not worth it.

T&R Cannabis does its best to appeal to a wide range of potential customers with a few low-cost and high-price options since it is the only store in the area. There are several powerful, Tetrahydrocannabinol (THC) heavy strains. More balanced strains meant for smoking throughout an evening are also popular, and there are even two strains very high in cannabidiol (CBD) while very low in THC, which are marketed toward people looking to use cannabis for medical reasons without getting very high.[VI] The Stevenson brothers got into the business because they love pot. Almost always, at least one of them is working. They have a wealth of knowledge and can provide great advice if you are willing to risk getting trapped listening to a ten-minute soliloquy about the history and merits of each and every strain.

While the Stevenson brothers are enthusiastic and knowledgeable purveyors of marijuana, their selection cannot compare to that of Indica Aficionado, which is famous for its bud selection. The store boasts not only more than 200

[V] This exactly how the requirement is stated in the Permanent Rules Related to the Colorado Retail Marijuana Code adopted on Sept 9, 2013. I suspect all states will eventually adopt this rule.

[VI] Tetrahydrocannabinol, also known as THC, is one of the several dozen cannabinoids naturally produced by marijuana. It is the primary psychoactive compound in marijuana, but other cannabinoids are known to significantly affect a smoker's experience. Cannabidiol is not directly psychoactive but responsible for some of marijuana's medical benefits.

different strains, but several different versions of some of the more popular strains. Connoisseurs believe that, like wine, the terroir of marijuana confers unique characteristics to plants that are otherwise genetically identical.[VII] Some competitors have been known to joke that Indica Aficionado was founded solely to prove that Napa Valley doesn't have a monopoly on pretentiousness. (Of course, the actual jokes tend to be much cruder than that, often focusing on the problems arising from inserting or removing heads from asses.)

In T&R Cannabis, large amounts of each strain are kept in large, locked transparent containers full of buds. Next to each container are a few pre-measured clear packages customers may grab for convenience, or they can have an employee open one of the large containers to measure out the desired amount and select the perfect buds. On each container is a sign listing the name of the strain as well as the price, where it was grown, the company that grows it, when it was harvested, the lot number, its percentage of each of the major cannabinoids, moisture content, what chemicals were used to grow it, what independent lab tested it for safety, and, of course, the FDA-required warning label. This same basic set of information must be provided for any marijuana or marijuana product sold in the country. If you look carefully at the label, you will notice that almost all of the buds are relatively local, with only a few high-end options from California and Colorado. The strain's name, price, percentage of THC and CBD, and whether it is certified

---

[VII] Terroir is a French term that loosely translates as a "sense of place." The same grapes grown in different regions will produce wines with different "personalities" due to the unique light, weather, and soil of a given region.

organic are all in large print—when it comes to buds, these are the properties that consumers tend to care most about. Location and name of the company tend to be in smaller print unless the product came from a particularly famous grower.

Buying buds is more like buying apples than beer or laundry detergent. Consumers are almost always allowed to inspect the buds directly or through clear packaging. They can directly judge the quality by examining the product's appearance and smell. This is different than the way people buy soda or a box of cereal—when buying a completely sealed good, a customer depends on familiarity with the brand for a guarantee of quality. This is a primary factor that has kept the market for buds relatively localized, diverse, and mostly free of large players. Other factors include the slow process by which marijuana was legalized and the rigid nature of many regulations.

When medical marijuana and finally recreational marijuana were first legalized at the state level, for many years they remained technically in violation of federal law. This legal gray area had several major effects. The first is that it kept the marijuana industry isolated from other corporate endeavors. No large company wanted to put its existing business in potential legal danger; getting involved in the marijuana sector was not worth the risk of having all assets seized by the federal government. Conversely, no business involved in the gray market for marijuana at the time ever expanded significantly into other industries.

In states that approved medical marijuana or legalization before the Regulation and Control of Cannabis Act, these risk-taking entrepreneurs had a huge advantage when federal prohibition ended. This meant that even after the federal law made it legally permissible for unrelated, large businesses to expand into the marijuana industry, the diverse, pre-existing market didn't make it easy. These established companies were also in a position to lobby for state regulations that would work to their advantage.

A similar dynamic was at play after the end of alcohol prohibition. The few wineries and distilleries that survived prohibition by selling "medical liquor" or "sacramental wine" were best positioned to take advantage of the ratification of the 21st Amendment. Many of these same brands are around to this day—for example, the Four Roses Bourbon brand survived prohibition thanks to being one of only six distilleries to get permission to legally produce bourbon for medical purposes. This market advantage helped make it the best-selling bourbon in the United States in the '30s and '40s following the ratification of the 21st Amendment.[19]

There was one critical distinction, however, between the gray marijuana market and the medical bourbon and sacramental wine markets decades earlier: During alcohol prohibition, the federal government approved only a few large medical bourbon distilleries and wineries, whereas no marijuana companies were licensed during this legal gray period. If a marijuana producer or retailer tried to operate in multiple states, it risked unwanted federal scrutiny over interstate commerce issues. This kept most marijuana businesses small and isolated to individual states.

Additionally, federal crackdowns on state medical marijuana programs or legal marijuana systems would often target the largest businesses. A marijuana company that grew too large in these gray-market days would often find itself made an example of by the federal government.

In its first term, the Obama administration effectively adopted a policy of going after the largest medical marijuana operations for violating federal law. In 2012, Michael Scherer in Time Magazine reported, "The federal government is not trying to eliminate medical marijuana altogether, but it has decided that it cannot stand for the commercialization or large scale production of marijuana for the stated purpose of helping the sick, even when that production is technically within the bounds of state law."[20] In a 2012 Rolling Stone interview, when asked about the crackdown on medical marijuana, President Obama strongly implied that federal officials were primarily targeting "large-scale, commercial operations."[21]

In 2011 and 2012, two of the largest and most prominent entities in California's medical marijuana system—Harborside Health Center and Oaksterdam University—were targeted by federal agencies for growing marijuana. At the same time, the federal government barely noticed the numerous small and significantly shadier dispensaries that were skirting the edges of state law. Harborside and Oaksterdam University both went to great lengths to fully comply with state law. It can only be concluded that the federal government wanted to make an example of them, given their large size and active role in publicly advocating for marijuana reform.

Steve DeAngelo, the executive director of Harborside, was about to star in the documentary series *Weed Wars* on the Discovery Channel when the IRS targeted the health center, claiming it could not deduct traditional business expenses since it made its money selling a drug that was illegal under federal law. For over a decade, since the first states approved medical marijuana, dispensaries had been filing their federal tax returns like any normal business, deducting traditional expenses like rent and payroll. It was only in 2011 that the IRS concluded that an anti-drug tax provision adopted in 1982 meant Harborside suddenly owed millions in back taxes.[22]

Similarly, in 2010, Oaksterdam University founder Richard Lee became a high-profile advocate for marijuana policy reform—he was the main sponsor of Proposition 19, a ballot measure in California to legalize marijuana that ultimately failed, 54 percent to 46 percent. Lee was in many ways the face of the campaign and became one of the most vocal activists in favor of legalization. Less than two years later, as new legalization campaigns were heating up in other states, the DEA and IRS raided Oaksterdam University and Lee's home.[23] The raids seemed to have the intended effect: Days later, Lee announced he would step down from running Oaksterdam University, an educational facility he founded in 2007 to train people in all aspects of the medical marijuana industry.

While Haborside was among the biggest medical marijuana dispensaries in California in 2011, it was still a relatively small operation. Harborside's yearly revenue was only in the low millions. They represented only a tiny percentage of the state's overall medical marijuana retail sales. During marijuana's weird legal limbo, while it was legal under state law but technically prohibited under federal law, most of the industry lived by the Japanese proverb, "the nail that sticks out gets hammered down."

One of the more overlooked but significant lasting impacts of marijuana prohibition on the bud business has to do with intellectual property law. In 1930, Congress adopted the Plant Patent Act, which first made it possible to patent varieties of domestic plants. Many of the more popular varieties of fruits, hops, and flowers in the United States have been patented and/or trademarked. For years, the University of Minnesota held the patent trademark on Honeycrisp apples, and it generated millions for the institution.[24] Yet while marijuana was illegal under federal laws, it was impossible for marijuana innovators to get these same protections. Products that are "immoral or scandalous," like illegal drugs, can't be registered with the Patent and Trademark Office.[25] As a result, hundreds of strains and many terms developed to describe marijuana effectively ended up in the public domain. Since federal legalization, several new strains have been patented, but it is tough to compete with so many popular strains that are freely available, such as White Widow, Maui Waui, Bubba Kush, Silver Haze, Northern Lights, etc.—all developed during prohibition.

Some early regulations also played a significant role in keeping the industry fractured by making it hard to start big brands or chains. Regulators feared the idea of "Big Marijuana" or a "Starbucks of Weed" and took steps prevent it. State regulations either directly prohibited large marijuana businesses or indirectly made them extremely difficult to develop.

Washington State's original recreational marijuana rules adopted in 2013 limited the number of licenses a business could have. According to the rules, "Any entity and/or principals within any entity are limited to no more than three retail marijuana licenses with no multiple location licensee allowed more than thirty-three percent of the allowed licenses in any county or city." The state restricted how large any one marijuana grow operation could be and set a similar three-license limit on growers.[26]

In addition, strict restrictions on advertising made it difficult to develop well known brands of bud. Marijuana is subject to strict controls by the Center for Cannabis Products, a division of the FDA modeled after the Center for Tobacco Products created in 2010. A marijuana business will lose its license to operate if it does not comply with rules regarding advertising. These rules closely mirror the restrictions put on cigarettes but in some cases go even further. Marijuana businesses can't advertise on any TV program, newspaper, radio, billboard, websites, etc. that is likely to be seen by a significant number of minors. You won't be seeing marijuana commercials during the Super Bowl, or sporting events held at Chill Buds Stadium. Event sponsorship and event-space naming rights are both prohibited. The incorporation of elements that could be interpreted as appealing to minors, such as cartoon characters, is also outlawed in advertising.

Extracts, Sprays, and Edibles

If you're not looking for the traditional buds on the right-hand wall of T&R Cannabis, behind the counter are all the other products containing THC. There are a few brands of pre-rolled joints, different varieties of hashish, a few types of THC lozenges and chews, pills, THC sprays, refills for marijuana extract vaporizers, and several varieties of THC-infused cooking oils. Hashish and marijuana concentrates must not exceed 80 percent cannabinoids by weight. Concentration beyond that level is considered dangerously intoxicating, so several states have set a hash ceiling for the same reason they banned alcohol over 151 proof (75.5 percent alcohol by volume).

One popular choice that has developed a national reach is Puget Chills' Pungent Suckers. The company, founded in 2015 in Tacoma, Washington, sells three different brands including regular strength (8 mg THC, 0.2 mg CBD, 0.1 mg CBN per lozenge), extra strength (10 mg THC, 0.2 mg CBD, 0.1 mg CBN) and extra chill (10 mg THC, 0.1 mg CBD, 0.2 mg CBN). Each packet contains ten lozenges. What really sets the company apart is that all of their lozenges are only flavored by one of their proprietary strains of cannabis bred for taste. This gave them a big advantage when the FDA started cracking down on "child-friendly" added flavors.

These niche THC products are where you tend to find significant brands. Yet even these markets are fairly diverse. Only in the past decade have true national companies actually emerged. Several marijuana companies from the gray legal era compete with a range of multi-national corporations and new start-ups to be the go-to brand for each of these marijuana product categories. Many venture capitalists dream of becoming the Heinz Ketchup of marijuana lozenges, but none have managed to grab a dominant market share. Contrary to some predictions and fears, marijuana hasn't been monopolized by a handful of large snack-food, alcohol, or tobacco conglomerates. Similarly, even though alcohol prohibition ended in 1933, real consolidation in the beer and alcohol industry took decades. Even then, high-level consolidation was a rather short-lived market condition created by bad regulation.

Heavy consolidation among a few big beer companies was not some natural end state created by the invisible hand of the market. It was a policy choice. The government adopted regulations that disadvantaged smaller producers and made new start-ups almost impossible. For example, most states didn't change their rules that prohibited "tied houses" until the 1980s. A tied house is a bar owned by a particular brewery, which sells that brewery's beer. This prevented brewers from selling directly to consumers, making it very difficult to start a new small brewery without a massive investment. In 1982, California helped kick off the micro-brewing revolution when it allowed breweries to sell directly to consumers as long as they maintained a restaurant on site. With brewpubs finally legal in California, many other states soon followed suit. Starting around the beginning of the 21st century, micro-brews and craft distilleries saw an explosion in popularity, thanks in large part to changes in regulation. In 1983, there were only 80 breweries in the United States, but by 1996, there were over 1,000 with new ones being founded every day.[27] Unlike the United States, Germany never experienced extreme market concentration in its beer industry, because the government made it a goal of its regulations to protect the country's long and diverse brewing tradition.

Allowing some limited "vertical integration" in the beer industry by small firms has made it easier for artisan breweries to start and stay viable. Finding an independent distributor and independent stores willing to carry a beer only produced in small batches with a limited fan base is very difficult compared to selling the beer directly to consumers. When Colorado first legalized marijuana, it actively encouraged small-scale vertical integration in the industry and even required it in the first few months. Washington State's original marijuana legalization law explicitly prohibited any form of vertical integration, but the first regulations were written to aggressively favor only small marijuana businesses by strictly capping how many licenses one company could have.

Any marijuana consumable sold in a store can't have a serving size that contains more than 10 mg of THC, and the individual package can't contain more than 100 mg total. Both Colorado and Washington State adopted this rule after legalization, and it became a national standard. (Regulators tend to follow precedent when possible and like round numbers.) The only consumables allowed in New Jersey are some uncolored, "adult flavored" lozenges and chews. There are no pot brownies for retail sale, although you can buy THC-infused cooking oil, and the staff at T&R Cannabis will happily give you advice on how to bake your own.

The FDA considers brightly colored foodstuffs, candy flavors, lollipops, ice cream, or baked goods containing THC to be troubling on several levels. These products seem to be marketed to individuals under the age of 21. There is also the risk of accidental ingestion by adults and young children unaware of the products' THC content. The federal government does not allow these products to be made for retail sale. After the FDA put these rules in place, a pair of senators from Vermont and Maine tried to quietly insert into the 2024 Farm Bill a special carve-out for pure maple syrup candies containing THC by classifying it as a natural binder and not a candy flavor. The treats were briefly popular with tourists in Vermont after the state legalized marijuana but before the federal government legalized it and the FDA started getting involved. But once it was discovered and subsequently dubbed "syrupgate" by the media and late-night comedians, the provision got stripped in committee.

You also won't be able to find any marijuana products that also contain alcohol, caffeine, tobacco, nicotine or other legal drugs, as mandated by the FDA. Marijuana extracts can be suspended in ethanol, but the ethanol can only be used as a solvent. The alcohol content must be low enough so that it doesn't amplify the intoxicating effects. While nothing legally prevents individuals from consuming these substances at the same time, retailers are prohibited from selling products that contain a mixture or co-packaging of intoxicants, and consumers are advised not to mix substances. Even before states started legalizing marijuana, the FDA set a precedent that products mixing legal drugs are unacceptably dangerous. After canned alcoholic drinks containing high levels of caffeine became popular in 2010, the FDA warned manufacturers that it considered the combination to be unsafe and forced the companies to stop selling the combination.[28] The mixture was linked to several deaths.

Paraphernalia

The small back wall of T&R Cannabis is mostly taken up by marijuana paraphernalia. Almost half the wall is dedicated to every type of rolling paper imaginable. There is also a decent of selection pipes, bongs, vaporizers, and, of course, lighters. By law, marijuana retailers in New Jersey and most other states can only sell marijuana and marijuana related products. The official justification is that there shouldn't be any reason for a minor to be in these stores or to receive anything from them. These rules are supported by other businesses, such as convenience stores and liquor retailers, that prefer not to face extra competition.

Most control states take this concept even further. Inside the Durham CCC store, the only items for sale are buds and a small selection of marijuana-infused products. There are no attractive display pieces from which you can select the exact weight of each strain you want. Employees are only helpful with basic issues but not exactly knowledgeable. This is just a job for them, not a passion. Buds are available only in premeasured, clear plastic boxes, which come only in four predetermined weights. Each box is equipped with a unique security chip so it can be tracked. Despite the less welcoming interior and less knowledgeable customer service, you can find some version of nearly every marijuana product sold at T&R Cannabis. The major difference is that the CCC store sells nothing to smoke your marijuana with. There is serious private sector and ideological opposition to anything that hints of government expansion of its retail business beyond its narrow mandate. (Conservatives eagerly point out that government-run businesses are technically socialism, the evils of which they consider to be self-evident.)

Meanwhile, the private sector has been quick to respond to the obvious demand. Right next door or across the street from nearly every CCC store, there is a convenience store/head shop selling any smoking device you could ask for. Since they don't sell marijuana, these shops can also sell tobacco products such as cigar wraps for rolling blunts.

At the counter of Indica Aficionado, you will notice that in addition to rolling papers you can find bottled water, breath mints, and eye drops in the prime location for impulse purchases. California has some of the laxest restrictions on what marijuana retailers can sell, but it still prohibits them from selling alcohol or tobacco products. As long as marijuana products make up 85 percent of the business, they're permitted to sell almost anything. Cannabis tourism is a booming industry in parts of California, and branded hats and shirts are very popular at stores like Indica Aficionado, which cater to this market.

Chapter 3 – Price

Browsing the many options can be fun, especially at a high-end store like Indica Aficionado, but if you actually want any marijuana, you'll need to pay for it. I would strongly advise against trying to shoplift. The prevalence of security cameras and radio-frequency identification tags required by the seed-to-sale tracking laws almost makes robbing a bank seem easy by comparison.

Let's say that at T&R Cannabis you've selected a one-ounce (28 grams) package of their organic, locally grown White Widow. Most customers tend to buy only an eighth of an ounce at a time, but buying a full ounce is not uncommon. Since an ounce is a standard measurement for several government policies, let's just pretend you need a lot of weed. This particular White Widow is one of the pricier top-shelf choices at the store.

The price tag says it costs \$76.30,[VIII] nearly identical to the \$73.41 price for a similar option at the CCC store in Durham.[IX]

All four White Widow options at Indica Aficionado cost 30 to 150 percent more, due to their unusually high quality. If you dare question the high price, one of Aficionado's cannabis sommeliers will helpfully explain to you in great detail the rare and valuable nature of their buds. One, for instance, is a proprietary version of the strain grown in a hydroponic setup with a mixture of natural sunshine and limited-wavelength OLED lights to provide an optimal level of stressing right before harvest, after which is subject to a secret curing process to enhance its flavor. If price is a problem for you, you'll be politely directed toward the less-refined retailers in the area where you'll find more mundane versions, priced more in line with the national average.

Risk Premium During Prohibition

Roughly \$75 dollars for an ounce of quality marijuana is either a very good deal or a very bad one, depending on your

---

[VIII] All prices in this book are listed in 2013 dollars. Adjusting for inflation would be needlessly confusing without adding any real value to readers, not to mention that if I could confidently predict Federal Reserve policy and macroeconomic conditions over the next two decades I would be doing something far more profitable than writing.

[IX] Uruguay has been considering setting a price for legal marijuana ranging from \$28 to \$71 an ounce.
Uruguay Will Sell Legal Marijuana For \$1 Per Gram, Official Says. Huffington Post. Oct 21, 2013.
http://www.huffingtonpost.com/2013/10/21/uruguay-marijuana-1-per-gram_n_4137179.html?utm_hp_ref=tw

perspective: It is significantly cheaper than marijuana ever was during its prohibition but noticeably more expensive than it theoretically could be were it not subjected to taxes, licensing fees, and regulation. When marijuana was illegal, a regular consumer would spend around four to ten times that price. According to the crowd-sourcing site PriceofWeed.com, in 2013 an ounce of "high quality" marijuana would cost on average around $360 in New Jersey. While prohibition was mostly a failure at stopping people from using marijuana, it did get a lot of people arrested, drove up prices, and helped make some lucky criminals very rich. Two of the main reasons marijuana was so much more expensive during prohibition were the risk premium and the inherent inefficiency that resulted from criminalization.

During the height of marijuana prohibition, someone growing or selling a significant amount of marijuana was taking many serious risks above and beyond what any legal business would, whose biggest possible risks are bankruptcy and loss of investment. An illicit business faced all the risks of a legal business in addition to some significant other risks.

Obviously, the biggest threat was getting caught. There was the real risk of being arrested, convicted, and sent to prison. Most people consider going to prison to be a very unpleasant experience. A person convicted of a serious drug crime will be forced to deal with the stigma of being a convicted felon, making it difficult to find employment, travel internationally, and maintain the right to vote.

There were many financial concerns as well: Mounting a legal defense can be expensive. In addition, being charged with a drug crime could result in asset forfeits—with or even without a conviction. Law enforcement would not only take the drugs, but they could also seize any assets that may have been used in or were the result of a drug crime. Cars, money, boats, homes, land, etc. were often seized as a result of drug arrests. Under civil asset forfeit laws in the United States, law enforcement agencies didn't even need to convict you of a drug violation before taking your possessions and reselling them for profit. When legal action is taken against a person's property rather than against the individual, there is normally a much lower standard of proof.

Even without the interference of law enforcement, the financial risks were high. For example, when someone in the black market had good reason to think they were about to get caught, they would dump their marijuana. Losing your inventory is not as bad as being arrested, but it is a still a big loss that legal businesses don't typically need to worry about. Simply not having access to the legal system also created and exacerbated risks. Criminals who rob someone engaged in an illicit trade don't usually have to worry that the victim will go to the police. A legal business could not only go to the cops, but often file an insurance claim to recover their losses as well. To make it worth taking these risks, the black market had to charge a significant premium above the regular production cost for marijuana.

Beyond the risks, the need to avoid law enforcement makes everything incredibly inefficient. Marketing, hiring, security, and accounting all become dramatically more difficult. Even the most basic task for a legal business can be a serious ordeal for a black-market business. Take something as simple as making a purchase. Buyers of an illegal product aren't going to use credit cards, checks, or direct bank deposits. Almost all transactions have to be in cash, which can be very cumbersome especially when dealing with large quantities. Illegal businesses can't simply deposit large amounts of cash in a bank—that would raise suspicion. The cash must be laundered, which adds a new layer of cost and risk. You have to be sure whoever is laundering your money will not just steal it. All these added complications can make for good plot twists in shows like "Weeds" or "Breaking Bad," but they make black markets extremely dangerous—as also demonstrated by shows like "Weeds" and "Breaking Bad."

Even basic tasks such as hiring and firing employees become very complicated as well. You can't just post an ad on an Internet job site that reads, "need regional manager for illegal business." A regular business can simply fire an employee who doesn't work out with little fear of retribution, whereas an illegal business needs to be very careful about it. A former employee might turn you in for a financial reward or leniency on crimes they've been accused of. Additionally, when marijuana was entirely illegal, only an idiot would have ordered large industrial equipment specially designed for processing marijuana. It would be like putting up a giant sign reading, "arrest me."

Legalization fixed these problems, causing costs to drop significantly. The price of marijuana in the United States dropped primarily in two stages. The first was when marijuana became legal for medical or recreational use at the state level but was still illegal under federal law. This significantly reduced the risk premium and inefficiencies but did not eliminate them. In California, with its well established and lax medical marijuana system, an ounce of high quality bud only cost around $250 in 2013.

The vast majority of marijuana arrests were made by local authorities under state law, so as long as a person followed the state's marijuana statutes their chance of being arrested was significantly reduced, but not completely eliminated: Marijuana was still illegal under federal law. Federal agencies still occasionally raided, harassed, seized the assets of, and arrested people who were legally operating under their state's laws. For example, during President Obama's first term, well over 200 federal raids were conducted targeting medical marijuana businesses, and hundreds of threatening letters were sent to landlords renting to medical marijuana businesses.[29]

The change in states' laws made it is easier for state-approved marijuana businesses to operate in a more efficient manner in some respects—companies could advertise, rent property, and for the most part operate out in the open like normal businesses. Yet the continuing federal prohibition against marijuana still created some major issues. For years, federal agencies pressured banks and credit card companies to stop taking accounts from medical marijuana businesses. This forced medical marijuana dispensaries to operate as cash businesses, creating problems for accounting, order fulfillment, payroll, and security. Also problematic was how the federal government interpreted section 280E of the tax code, which was adopted in 1982 as a way to target drug traffickers by preventing them from qualifying for the standard deductions legitimate businesses benefit from. Since marijuana was still a Schedule I substance under federal law, medical marijuana dispensaries could have been subjected to effective federal income tax rates exceeding 70 percent.[30]

The next significant drop in price came after the federal government adopted the Regulation and Control of Cannabis Act, making marijuana fully legal in the states that allowed it. Finally, the marijuana industry could operate like any other business without any risk of arrest or asset seizure by federal agencies. This allowed the industry to become more efficient and professional. However, this second drop in price would have been much larger if not for regulations, licensing fees, and large excise taxes designed to keep the price high.

Cost of Regulations

If marijuana was barely regulated and only lightly taxed like, say, tomatoes or basil, the price could drop significantly. Cannabis is just a plant that in the right condition can grow like a weed—hence the nickname. High-quality bud does require some work: It needs optimal conditions, with the males separated from the females, and harvesting and trimming the buds is a time-intensive, hands-on process. But these factors account for only a small share of marijuana's overall retail price. Without the heavy government involvement, marijuana would probably retail for around the same price as other specialty agricultural goods that require intensive production and have similar characteristics. A close comparison would be a product like high-quality white tea, which requires individuals to hand-pluck only the youngest leaves. Its sells for a retail price of about $4-$9 an ounce. Perhaps an even better comparison might be quality cigars. Without federal and state excise taxes, good cigars would sell for the equivalent of $10-$15 an ounce, but very high quality ones can go much higher.[X]

Producing good marijuana buds is relatively labor-intensive, but it's nothing compared to saffron, the most expensive spice on the market. Usually, saffron is handpicked from the tiny stigmas of a flower, small hair-like threads at the center. Each flower only produces three stigmas at a time, and it takes several hundred threads to make just a single gram of saffron. Depending on quality, you will easily pay $100-$300 an ounce. The fact that marijuana used to sell for more than saffron during prohibition illustrates how drastically the black market drove up the price.

Of course, marijuana is highly regulated and taxed, which keeps the price higher than it theoretically could be. The government has four objectives regarding legal marijuana that keep the price high:

1. They want to keep it away from minors.

2. They want to extract significant revenue from it. This requires high taxes and efforts to stop tax evasion.

[X] A 2010 Rand working paper that looked at the likely labor and production costs in the marijuana industry if Proposition 19 had passed concluded a well-run one-acre greenhouse operation might be able to produce marijuana for around $6-$16 per ounce.
Caulkins, Jonathan P. Estimated Cost of Production for Legalized Cannabis. Rand. July 2010.
http://www.rand.org/content/dam/rand/pubs/working_papers/2010/RAND_WR764.pdf

3. They want to keep it from being diverted to the black market in places that have not legalized it. This goal has lost some significance as more places legalize it.

4. They want to discourage consumption, and higher prices are one way to do that.

One of the prime ways in which the government advances the first three goals is by requiring extensive monitoring and security systems. These also add to the cost of production, which helps advance the fourth goal. The whole industry is subject to a form of "seed to sale" monitoring that was pioneered in Colorado first for medical marijuana and then recreational marijuana. The basic idea is that every marijuana product is carefully monitored, recorded, and audited from the moment the seed is planted to the time the consumer leaves the store. Since its early days, the concept has been refined and expanded as new technology has made the process easier and more comprehensive. Progressively better and more affordable cameras and automatic tracking equipment have streamlined the system.

The high taxes on legal marijuana and the premium on marijuana in places where it is illegal mean that it is theoretically possible to make a decent profit on the illegal sale of marijuana if you can sidestep the legal system. Intensive monitoring ensures the excise taxes are paid on each step of the process and that nothing disappears out the backdoor or off the back of a truck.

Marijuana is not grown out in the open like corn—you won't see endless fields of marijuana loaded down with buds ready for harvest while driving down the highway. Most people will never see a commercial marijuana plant unless they take one of the special cannabis estate tours that have become popular in Northern California and Vermont. Like winery and brewery tours, they give people a chance to see the process and sample the products.

As per government regulation, cannabis must be grown in a secured location, either an enclosed space or a properly fenced-off field with security cameras. Nor can just anyone work in the industry—every employee must be 21 and pass a criminal background check. At every step of the process, the product must be weighed, diligently recorded, and reported to the proper enforcement agencies. Even the waste from the plants must be accounted for and treated so that it becomes unusable. Each individual package of marijuana in a store must be equipped with an electronic tracking tag for inventory audits and to prevent shoplifting. Every step is subject to random audits. Violations can result in significant fees, loss of business licenses, and even criminal charges in egregious cases.

If you look closely at the package of White Widow you selected in T&R Cannabis, you will notice the unique identifying number in small print on the electronic tracking tag: 30NJP9786L023U003475. This indicates year, state, producer, lot number, and individual unit. With this number, a government official with access to the New Jersey Department of Cannabis Enforcement can tell you the entire history of the buds you just bought. They know where the bud was grown, the day it was planted, the specific section of field it was grown in, when the two mandatory independent safety tests were done, and roughly the hour it was harvested. It is even possible to determine which four employers were on shift when these buds were trimmed and the name of the driver who delivered it to the store.

You will also notice if you look around T&R Cannabis that the place is blanketed with cameras—but they're well hidden among the tacky '60s decorations. The cameras are of course much easier to spot at the CCC store in Durham, which makes no attempt to hide them. That would detract from the DMV-like vibe the place has carefully cultivated.

T&R Cannabis uses one camera each to monitor outside the front as well as the back of the store. At the front door, there are three used as part of the ID verification process. Four cameras monitor every inch of merchandise, and another two directed at the counter scan the exchange of money and the customer making the purchase. Unseen in the back are another four that monitor inventory and deliveries. As you can see, trying to steal from a marijuana store is a really stupid idea.

The cost of these background checks, security features, and monitoring systems are shouldered by the producers and retailers, who in turn pass them on to consumers in the form of slightly higher prices, but it is the taxes which really push up the cost for people using marijuana.

Chapter 4 - Taxes

Once you pay for your ounce of White Widow at T&R Cannabis, one of the employees will put it in an opaque plastic container with a reusable childproof top. The only markings on this case are two warning labels. This time you get "WARNING: Marijuana can impair concentration, coordination, and judgment. Do not operate a vehicle or machinery under the influence of this drug" and "WARNING: This product has intoxicating effects and may be habit forming. Smoking is hazardous to your health."[XI] Both Washington State and Colorado adopted nearly identical regulations that required opaque, child-resistant containers when they became the first states to legalize recreational marijuana, and, like many

---

[XI] These are two of the warnings adopted by Washington State after legalization.
Initiative 502 Adopted Rules. Washington State Liquor Control Board. Oct 16, 2013 http://lcb.wa.gov/marijuana/initiative_502_proposed_rules

marijuana policy decisions made by these two states, these rules became the basis for a national standard.

You will now be handed your package, your change, and a receipt. You may notice that the only tax listed is the 7 percent state tax, which brought your $76.30 purchase to $81.64. Similarly, if you buy buds in Oakland, there is a 7 percent state sales tax plus a 2 percent local tax, while at the CCC store in Durham, state and local taxes will add 7.5 percent. While these same rates are applied to almost all consumer goods, in the case of marijuana these sales taxes represent only a small fraction of the portion of your purchase that went to the government. The bulk of government revenues from recreational marijuana come from licensing fees and excise taxes that are hidden from regular consumers.

If you want to run any type of marijuana business, you must pay local and federal licensing fees. There are different fees for every step of the process: fees for the grower, for the processer, for shippers, and for retailers. Most states even have a fee for individual employees to cover the cost of state-run background checks. When you start your weed business, there is usually a large, one-time application fee as well as an annual license renewal fee to remain in operation. These fees can be significant, often costing thousands of dollars a year depending on the scope of the license. Colorado's original recreational marijuana regulations adopted in 2013 required a $5,000 application fee for new marijuana-related businesses. This was in addition to the operational licensing fee, which, depending on the type and size of the marijuana business, ran from $2,750 to $14,000 annually. Some of the nation's highest marijuana licensing fees for medical marijuana were in Massachusetts, where in 2013 the state's Department of Public Health instituted a $31,500 application fee and a $50,000 annual registration fee for dispensaries.[31]

While these large licensing fees bring in a modest amount of money, the bulk of the government's revenue from legal marijuana comes from the high excise taxes. Marijuana is considered a legal vice, like alcohol, tobacco, and gambling. Like these other vices, pot is subject to a substantial "sin tax." Once all federal and state taxes are factored in, taxes make up over half of what you are paying for that that ounce of White Widow. Of the $81.64 you paid at the T&R Cannabis, roughly $45 went to the government in the form of taxes.

While this tax rate may seem massive, it is not out of line with how alcohol and tobacco are treated in many places. For example, in Oregon, which is a liquor control state, if you bought a bottle of hard alcohol in 2012, roughly 50 percent of the cost went to the government—13.6 percent went to the federal excise tax and another 37 percent in "profit" was returned to state and local governments.[32] The Distilled Spirits Council of the United States claims that in 2012, "direct alcohol excise and sales taxes levied at the federal, state, and local levels account for more than one-third of the shelf price of many popular brands."[33]

Cigarettes face an even higher tax rate in most of the country than hard alcohol. In 2010 roughly 53 percent of the average retail price of a pack of cigarettes in the United States was due to excise taxes and fees related to the tobacco companies' settlements with state governments. In certain parts of the country, like New York City, the rate was even higher: 62 percent.[34] Yet, by international standards, that is still low.

According to the World Health Organization, in 2012 there were more than 30 countries where the taxes on cigarettes were so high they constituted over 70 percent of the retail price of a pack.[35]

Tax revenues generated from marijuana are split roughly 35 percent to 65 percent between federal and local governments. This standard divide is due in part to the fact that recreational cannabis was first legalized and taxed in multiple states before the federal government ended prohibition. Several states came to depend on their high marijuana taxes and did not want to lose this revenue to the federal government. At the same time, they didn't want their local marijuana industry and marijuana tax base undermined by cheap marijuana from neighboring states with lower marijuana taxes. This tax question was by far the most contentious issue surrounding the Regulation and Control of Cannabis Act of 2022 and came close to derailing the bill several times. Regardless of the issue, money is almost always at the center of any political fight.

Eventually, a novel compromise was reached to establish relatively uniform marijuana prices across the nation, without costing states their marijuana revenue: The federal government essentially created a two-part excise tax system. The first part consisted of standard excise taxes that would apply to all marijuana products sold in the country to help fund the federal government. The second part encouraged states to adopt their own high excise taxes. Marijuana faces this additional federal excise tax only if it isn't subjected to an equal or larger local tax/surcharge. Basically, any amount of local marijuana taxes could be deducted from this part of the federal tax. If a state chose not to tax marijuana at all, the marijuana was still taxed, and the tax revenue went entirely to the federal government. This system has convinced all green states to adopt a high excise tax, and it has effectively allowed the federal government to set a minimum price for marijuana in the country.

To make legalization ballot initiatives more appealing, many states included provisions that allotted tax revenue from marijuana to unrelated, popular social programs. Amendment 64 in Colorado specifically required that the first $40 million in annual revenue raised from marijuana taxes go to its public school construction assistance fund. Initiative 502 in Washington State required part of its marijuana tax revenue to be spent on public insurance programs and substance-abuse treatment. In several redder states, in order to garner Republican support in the state legislature, ballot initiatives proposed that marijuana tax revenue would be used for a dollar-for-dollar reduction in state income taxes or general sales taxes. Slogans like 'tax potheads instead of hard work' really resonated with certain voters.

Why Taxes Are So High

Marijuana reform activists: For activists in the early days, the prospect of tax revenues from legal marijuana served two important functions: Primarily, it was a strong talking point in selling the idea of legalization to older voters, non-users, and other skeptics of reform who had no reason to support legalization otherwise. Many of the early campaigns focused on this tax message hard. Every TV ad run by the campaign behind Initiative 502 in Washington State mentioned the revenue legal marijuana could generate.[36] Secondly, the marijuana tax made it that much harder for governments to overturn legalization. Without significant tax revenue, it would be easier for a new governor or ballot initiative campaign to re-criminalize it in the future. On the other hand, politicians would be loath to raise taxes or cut spending on other programs to make up for the revenue lost in re-criminalizing marijuana. The same dynamic hampered the push for national alcohol prohibition until the ratification of the 16th Amendment in 1913, which authorized a federal income tax. Before then, liquor taxes generated as much as 40 percent of the federal government's annual revenue, which made alcohol prohibition financially impossible until this new revenue source could be tapped.[37] It's no wonder, then, that the Anti-Saloon League was a big supporter of the 16th Amendment as part of its long-term plan to get the 18th Amendment passed.

This strategy proved remarkably effective. As legalization spread through the states, it was one thing for politicians to say they were against marijuana use, but it was quite another to blow a massive hole in a state's budget. The much-needed influx of funds also made some politicians in the early states more willing to push back against the federal governments' attempts to harass newly approved marijuana retailers.

Marijuana reform activists borrowed this tactic directly from anti-alcohol prohibition activists almost a century earlier. During the Great Depression, both federal and local government revenue dropped along with incomes. The potential for revenue and job creation were two of the most prominent political talking points employed by anti-prohibition campaigners. In 1932, New York Mayor James Walker managed to get over 100,000 people to march in the "Beer for Taxation" parade.[38]

Liberals looking for social welfare support: Liberals have traditionally been the group most supportive of marijuana legalization. In 2011, Gallup found only 50 percent of Americans supported marijuana legalization, while 69 percent of liberals did. Liberals also tend to support more spending on government programs, so they were more than happy to use high marijuana taxation to raise money for social welfare. Legalization was a way to kill two birds with one stone. Most early state marijuana laws allotted a certain amount of marijuana tax revenue to particular liberal priorities such as education or health care.

Neutral politicians: Local politicians without a particularly strong stance on the issue of legalization were more than happy to accept the financial windfall. Unlike the federal government, local governments and states with balanced budget requirements don't have the luxury of running deficits. Budget fights are often the most brutal and least enjoyable part of local politics. When presented with an easy way to raise substantial revenue that would be acceptable to the vast majority of voters, many local politicians jumped at the chance. This pattern was already evident even when marijuana was legalized only in a few states for medical purposes. For example, in 2011, to help close a budget gap, the state of Oregon generated an extra $6.7 million by raising the registration fee for medical marijuana patients. Similarly, in 2010 the city of Oakland, California, tripled the tax it had placed on medical marijuana dispensaries to help deal with budget problems.[39]

Health policy experts: When marijuana legalization efforts began to pick up steam, public health experts held mixed opinions about the policy change, but they were in near-unanimous agreement that if marijuana was going to be legalized, the price should be artificially increased through taxes as a way to discourage excessive consumption. Like most goods, marijuana demand is price elastic: The more it costs, the less people are likely to buy. Public health advocates used similar reasoning in support of artificially high prices for cigarettes to discourage smoking.

Competing industries: Alcohol companies saw and continue to see marijuana as a competitive threat to their business. They know some people would rather relax after work with a joint than a glass of wine or a bottle of beer. During the 2010 Proposition 19 campaign, the California Beer & Beverage Distributors was one of the largest donors against the legalization initiative.[40] Once it became undeniable that legalization was inevitable, the alcohol industry had a clear incentive to make sure marijuana faced a tax rate at least as high or much higher than their own. Additionally, in many states, with fees from marijuana helping to finance the same regulatory agencies that regulate alcohol, the alcohol industry quietly argued that its fees should be reduced.

The Weak Opposition to High Taxes

Marijuana users: Even though users of marijuana are the most likely to oppose taxes, there was little opposition to taxation in the community when the drug was first being legalized. For the most part, marijuana users were so overjoyed by legalization that they quickly resigned themselves to paying high taxes on it and worked to ensure the community was on-message about accepting taxation as a way to promote legalization to the general public. In 2012, the marijuana legalization initiatives put on the ballot in Colorado, Washington, and Oregon by reform supporters all contained provisions calling for marijuana to be taxed. In Oregon, the campaign name of the legalization initiative was even titled the "Oregon Cannabis Tax Act." That measure narrowly lost, 47 percent yes to 53 percent no. Most importantly, legal marijuana—even with the large taxes and fees placed on it—is still cheaper than marijuana during prohibition.

Generating serious political opposition requires an organized campaign to harness popular opinion. Such campaigns are normally run by community activists and/or bankrolled by the affected industry. In the case of marijuana, most activists were promoting heavy taxes to make legalization more popular, and there was technically no pre-existing legal recreational marijuana industry to bankroll an anti-tax campaign.

Even if some marijuana users opposed a high excise tax in the early days of legalization, it didn't make a big impact. Marijuana users were and will always be a minority of the population, and it's always easier for the majority to impose taxes on a minority, especially when it comes to a vice. This is why from 1990 to 2010, one of the smoothest agreements the government arrived at was to raise taxes on cigarettes. In the ten-year period between 2002 and 2012, states and U.S. territories increased their cigarette taxes over 105 times.[41] It was a popular way to both reduce smoking and pay for new programs, such as the State Children's Health Insurance Program, which was expanded with cigarette-tax funding in 2009.

In 2011, roughly 19 percent of American adults smoked cigarettes regularly.[42] By comparison, in 2013, only about 7 percent of Americans said they currently smoked marijuana.[43] Marijuana was an even easier target for taxes than cigarettes ever were.

The marijuana industry: Of course, by definition, there wasn't a true recreational marijuana industry in place before legalization, which meant there was no well-established industry lobby to fight against high taxes on newly legalized recreational cannabis. The closest equivalent to an established industry was medical marijuana in states with licensed dispensaries, such as Colorado, California, Maine, and Washington. But even in these states, the medical marijuana industry was not a major force opposing taxes. Legalization in Colorado demonstrated that much of the industry shared the opinion of marijuana activists that taxation was useful for building lasting political support, and ultimately to the industry's benefit. In 2012, Amendment 64 legalized marijuana, but as a result of a provision in Colorado's constitution, the proposed excise tax on recreational marijuana needed to be approved separately. Amendment 64 merely gave the legislature the task of coming up with an official tax plan after the measure was approved by voters. The legislature agreed to create a 15 percent excise tax and a special 10 percent sales tax, but according to the constitution, a tax increase like this in Colorado must first be approved by the voters. So, the legislature put it on the 2013

November ballot as Proposition AA. (Yes, this insanely convoluted set of constitutional requirements was honestly how it worked.)

This bizarre circumstance gave the marijuana industry a chance to have their cake and eat it too: After marijuana was legalized based on the promise of new taxes, the industry had a chance to fight the actual tax provision separately. While a few in the medical marijuana industry tried to fight Prop. AA, the Medical Marijuana Industry Group, the largest industry group in the state, and the UFCW, the most important labor union in the industry, both actively endorsed it.[44]

Proposition AA ended up being approved 65 percent yes to 35 percent no. Much of the new revenue generated was set aside to fund schools. The year before, Amendment 64 only got a 55 percent yes vote. There was more support for taxing marijuana than there was for legalizing it. As it so happens, the 2013 ballot in Colorado also contained a different initiative that would have modestly raised income taxes to increase spending on education. This measured failed by a margin of almost two-to-one. The 2013 election perfectly demonstrated that increasing taxes on marijuana is politically one of the easiest ways to raise revenue.

Related businesses such as grow-kit suppliers, pipe manufacturers, rolling-paper companies, etc. also shared this basic position. Legalization was a financial boon, and taxes wouldn't directly affect them.

Conservatives and Republicans: Republicans and conservatives tend to be the biggest opponents of any tax increase, but as a group, conservatives were also the least supportive of marijuana use and legalization. In 2011, only 34 percent of self-identified conservatives and 35 percent of Republicans supported marijuana legalization.[45] As a result, conservative leaders and activists simply weren't invested in keeping taxes low on marijuana. Even if they tried, it would have been very difficult to rally their base for a pro-marijuana effort. Sin taxes are one of the few taxes for which it is possible to get Republican support. In 2009, 40 House Republicans voted for the bill funding the State Children's Health Insurance Program, which included a tax increase on tobacco products.[46]

Large excise taxes on newly legalized marijuana was one of the few sources of new revenue that could generate significant bipartisan support, thanks to in large part to Grover Norquist, the founder of Americans for Tax Reform. He was one of the most influential political activists in the country for decades. One of the main reasons Republicans refuse to support new taxes is that, since 1986, almost all elected Republicans signed the Americans for Tax Reform pledge to oppose any tax increases. The pledge helped to define the Republican Party at the start of the 21st century. Importantly, Norquist declared that imposing excise taxes on newly legalized marijuana is "not a tax increase. It's legalizing an activity and having the traditional tax applied to it."[47] He basically gave Republicans permission to vote for marijuana taxes, creating one source of new government revenue that was politically easier for Republicans to agree to.

How the Taxes Work

There are as many different marijuana tax schemes as there are states that have legalized it, but in general there are three ways the government approaches sin taxes: taxing based on a percentage of the price, taxing by quantity, and profiting directly off a government-run monopoly.

Tax based on price: This is how the federal excise tax on pistols works. As of 2013, the industries faced a special 10 percent sales tax.[48] When Colorado and Washington State became the first states to legalize marijuana, they used this basic system: The excise tax was a percentage of the wholesale and retail price of marijuana.

Several states use this system for at least part of their marijuana tax. The clear benefits are that it is simple and easy to enforce. It can be applied to pure marijuana and to marijuana-containing products. The big drawback is that it encourages cheap, low-quality weed. The cheaper a company can produce and sell marijuana, the lower the total tax placed on it will be. This gives cheaply grown, low-quality marijuana a double-price advantage: With low-priced, low-quality marijuana, you're also paying significantly less tax on the same amount of THC compared to higher-priced, high-quality buds.

Price-based taxation works against the goal of discouraging consumption, since companies are compelled to keep quality and prices low. From a public health perspective, there's also a disadvantage in that it can result in people inhaling more burnt plant material. And of course, from a connoisseur's perspective, a system that encourages low-quality weed is a bad one.

Tax by quantity: Many see a better way to structure a sin tax in taxing the content rather than the price. In this system, there's no advantage to a cheaper, low-quality product. This is how the federal government has set up most of its excise taxes for tobacco and alcohol. In 2013, the federal tax on cigarettes was $1.01 a pack. Similarly, the federal excise tax on distilled liquor was based on the amount of alcohol it contained. All standard 750-ml bottles of 80-proof alcohol faced a $2.14 tax, regardless of price.

To understand why from a public health perspective this type of tax is often considered a better option than a price-based tax, imagine two different packs of cigarettes—one a cheap, low-quality brand called Shitty Smokes and the other a high-end brand called Gold Deluxe. Shitty Smokes cost only $0.55 a pack before taxes, but Gold Deluxe is priced at $1.80. With a $1.01 per package tax applied, the price of Shitty Smokes would increase to $1.56 and Gold Deluxe would cost $2.81. By comparison, if the excise tax was simply a 100 percent sales tax, Shitty Smokes would only cost $1.10, and Gold Deluxe would cost $3.60. Under the second scheme Shitty Smokes are much cheaper, which encourages their consumption. People using Shitty Smokes are paying much less per pack even though the social/public health cost per pack is the same, if not slightly worse. If you to want to artificially increase the price, an excise tax based on quantity is best.

There are two ways to tax marijuana based on quantity. The first is a tax based on the weight of the usable buds. Some of the early marijuana legalization proposals at the beginning of the 21st century recommended a tax of $50 per ounce. Just one example was the Marijuana Control, Regulation, and Education Act, a bill put forward by California State Assembly member Tom Ammiano (D) in 2009. The bill was meant to raise awareness but not expected to pass.

The issue with a per-ounce tax is that it creates too many practical problems. There are too many ways to game this system, and with a large tax, plenty of incentive to try. Someone could remove only the trichomes[XII] from the buds to create very potent kief. This higher THC-per-ounce product would be a way to avoid most of the tax. It would be impractical to try to establish a legally enforceable standard of how well-trimmed a bud can be before it is no longer legally a bud. Dealing with products that contain marijuana would also be nearly impossible, with no way to independently verify that the stated weight of marijuana used in a product is accurate.

The most practical way to tax marijuana by quantity is to tax based on its THC content. This is the system the federal government adopted for marijuana, and it is used by most states. The federal government set the tax at $0.32 per 100 mg of THC. This tax doesn't necessarily favor cheaper marijuana, and it can be applied evenly to all marijuana-containing products and extracts. It also allows the federal government to set a clear floor on the cost of getting high.

Government monopoly with profits: The final way the government makes extra revenue from "sins" is by giving itself a monopoly and setting a high price that results in profits. The most obvious example is state lotteries. Most state-run lotteries generate significant profits, which are earmarked for particular government programs such as education. In 2012, the 44 states that had lotteries made over $19 billion off their programs.[49]

[XII] Trichomes are little hair structures on buds that tend to have the highest concentrations of THC.

The same is true in alcohol and marijuana control states. In alcohol control states, the government agency responsible chooses a markup high enough to allow for significant profits. While not technically a "tax," this is a cost being added to the product by the government, which receives the revenue directly. Oregon, for example, is a control state that doesn't bother with a liquor tax. Instead, it uses a markup to generate the profit that other states normally make from a liquor excise tax. Other control states, including North Carolina and Virginia, have an official liquor tax, and the products are also subject to a markup by government monopolies that earn a profit for the state. While this profitable markup may walk like a duck and quack like a duck, it benefits politically and legally from technically not being a duck. Since it is not a tax, the government has more legal flexibility. Raising the markup doesn't present the higher legal hurdles a tax increase would. It allows anti-tax Republicans to get revenue increases without violating their promise not to vote for new taxes.

Taxes in Action

Let's examine how these taxes actually work in practice with some simple examples. That ounce of White Widow you bought is 16.2 percent THC. What this means is that the 28.35 grams of bud you bought contains 4,593 mg of THC. In New Jersey, marijuana is subject to both the federal excise tax of $0.32 per 100 mg of THC and the New Jersey excise tax of $0.54 per 100 mg of THC. Note: The marijuana is not subject to the additional federal excise tax of $0.46 per 100 mg of THC because New Jersey's state excise tax is higher.

The producer sells the ounce to the retailer for $21. The federal excise tax of $14.70 and the state sales tax of $24.80 are applied at this point. This means that T&R Cannabis pays $60.5, but they can get refunded for the excise taxes if the product is not sold After their markup to cover payroll, rent, licenses, etc. T&R Cannabis sells the ounce for $76.30. After the 7 percent sales tax is applied, the final price you pay is $81.64. The government generated roughly $45 off your purchase from varies taxes.

The North Carolina CCC uses a very different tax structure, but it produces a similar result. They also buy an ounce of White Widow for $21 from the producer. At this point, the $14.70 federal tax is applied as well as a 75-cent bailment charge. The Local CCC board then subjects it to a 40 percent markup, bringing the price to $51.03. The state's 37 percent excise tax brings it to $69.91. Finally, an additional 5 percent markup for profit distribution is applied, and this ounce is given a shelf price of $73.41. When the sales tax is applied, you end up paying $78.91.[XIII] The system is very different, but the result is similar. Since the government markup/excise tax is high enough, the alternative federal tax doesn't apply.

The bulk of these taxes are purposefully hidden from you to make them more palatable, and it works. Most people have no idea how much in taxes was really applied to the last bottle of whiskey or case of beer they bought. Regular people care

---

[XIII] This pricing is roughly based on the North Carolina ABC's explanation of spirituous liquor pricing breakdown.
Spirituous Liquor Pricing Breakdown. ABC Commission North Carolina.
http://abc.nc.gov/pricing/breakdown.aspx

more about how much something costs them than the tax rate it is invisibly subjected to. Even with the government taking such a big share, marijuana is still a very affordable activity for adults. One gram of quality bud is more than enough to keep an average adult entertained for an evening, and that will cost you less than $3.00, even with all the taxes. That's still cheaper than going out to a movie, a six-pack of beer, or even just one cocktail at most bars.

Chapter 5 – Home Growing

After seeing just how significantly taxes and licensing fees have taken a bite out of your wallet, you might naturally be thinking, "Is there any legal way to avoid these taxes?" If you're in North Carolina, you're stuck with the CCC store as your only legal option. If you are in California, New Jersey, or one of the other 24 states that allow home growing, the answer is yes. However, you may quickly find out growing your own weed is not an effective way to save money.

Just because something is legal to own and use doesn't necessarily mean the government will allow you to produce it. It wasn't until 1978, a full 45 years after the 21st Amendment was ratified, that Congress finally legalized making small amounts of beer at home for personal use. Even then, states had the right to keep home brewing illegal, and several conservative states did so well into the 21st century. As late as 2012, Alabama was still actively enforcing its anti-home brewing laws. On September

20, 2012, three agents from the Alabama Alcoholic Beverage Control Board took $7,000 of brewing equipment from Hop City Craft Beer and Wine because they violated the state's laws against home brewing.[50] It wasn't until 2013 that Mississippi and Alabama finally became the last two states to legalize making limited amounts of beer at home, and they only legalized home brewing in their "wet" counties.[51] That meant that in Mississippi, for example, it was still illegal to make beer at home in the roughly half of the state that was still dry. Distilling spirits at home remains illegal anywhere in the country under federal law.

When states started legalizing medical marijuana, many decided to keep home growing illegal. While the medical marijuana laws in California, Hawaii, and Michigan all allowed home cultivation, the original medical marijuana laws in Delaware, New Hampshire, and Illinois prohibited it. This pattern repeated itself when states began to legalize recreational marijuana. In 2012, Colorado's marijuana legalization ballot measure allowed all adults to engage in limited home growing, but the initiative approved by voters in Washington State kept home cultivation illegal for non-medical marijuana patients. The states that prohibited home cultivation were primarily concerned about the black market, minors getting easier access, potential health hazards, and a loss of tax revenue.

In the 26 states where it is legal to grow marijuana at home, the rules regulating home growing vary significantly. In some states it is relatively easy, while in others the process is very involved. Several places require "hobby" growers to register with the state and pay a small fee to make up for lost tax revenue. Depending on the state, hobby growing is restricted to three to fifteen mature plants at a time. [XIV] The yearly harvest of only a handful of mature marijuana plants should produce enough marijuana to meet anyone's personal needs. Most states require anyone growing recreational marijuana for personal use do it in an "enclosed locked space" away from public view. Colorado set this precedent with Amendment 64. Even in states where you can grow your own marijuana, making your own hash oil is illegal for safety reasons. The most common method for making hash oil involves flammable solvents, such as butane, which be very dangerous if used incorrectly. Several people have blown up their homes and started fires trying to make hash oil. Hot, volatile chemicals are very dangerous outside a controlled professional setting.

Growing more than the personal limit is technically considered commercial production, and doing so without the proper license can result in being charged with several crimes, including unauthorized production and tax evasion. The debate over the appropriate legal boundary between a hobby and a commercial business is one of the always-changing, low-level legal issues that attend not just marijuana but also the home production of most other commercial products. The reality is that home growers are rarely arrested or charged with tax evasion for merely exceeding the personal grow limit by a few plants, if it is clear that the individual is a hobbyist. The laws are meant to prohibit only truly commercial unlicensed operations.

[XIV] Three to fifteen plants is the current range instituted by medical marijuana laws. As of 2013, Alaska, Colorado, Hawaii, Maine, and Nevada limited medical marijuana patients to three mature plants. Washington State has the highest limit with fifteen plants.

Prosecutions tend to be reserved for individuals who significantly exceed the limits.

In this way, the laws regulating marijuana home growing have some similarities to the restrictions placed on home alcohol brewing. Under federal law, a single adult household can legally produce up to 100 gallons of beer a year without paying taxes on it, as long as the beer is not sold. That is equal to 800 pints of beer a year for each adult—less than three beers a day. A few states have set their own, tighter restrictions. In Alabama you can only brew up to 15 gallons a year without paying taxes on it.[52] No one is ever arrested by the federal government for brewing 120 gallons of beer a year instead of the 100-gallon limit. Only egregious violations invite legal action.

Even if home growing is allowed under state law, some local ordinances prohibit it. Just as putting up a basketball hoop in your driveway or raising a chicken in your backyard can run afoul of local nuisance ordinances, so can growing marijuana. Many towns ban marijuana home growing due to the smell.

Why Home Cultivation Doesn't Hurt Tax Revenue

Marijuana legalization has allowed tens of thousands of enthusiasts to legally grow their own cannabis for personal use, yet it remains a small niche hobby practiced by relatively few adults. During the fight to legalize marijuana, some argued that allowing home cultivation would decimate state excise tax revenue, yet these fears proved to be unfounded. Even at the time, such an argument should have been laughable given how Americans treated other products subject to excise taxes, like alcohol and tobacco. It is possible to produce either product at home legally to avoid not only taxes but also corporate profits, but almost no one does. It doesn't fit human nature or make economic sense.

Financially, home cultivation just to avoid taxes is not worth it. The average marijuana user consumes only about 3.53 ounces a year,[53] or about three joints a week.[XV] Growing your own instead of buying saves you about $150 a year on taxes, which is quickly eaten up by the expenses involved in growing.

Let's say you want to grow at home. You might opt to do it in a locked greenhouse, which will set you back at least $500 if you go for the cheapest model. If you want to grow inside your house, you'll probably need a grow light, which will cost around $100 to buy and will add to your electric bill. Indoor growing requires ventilation and often a dehumidifier. If you happen to live in a densely populated area or an apartment, smell will be an issue. Depending on your local ordinances, the terms of your lease, and the tolerance of your neighbors, you could be forced to buy a quality air filter system that will not come cheaply. At minimum you'll need pots, soil, and fertilizer. If you want to grow some really good stuff, though, you'll probably need to invest in a hydroponic system. A cheap setup runs around $50 for a single plant. Once you factor in the cost of equipment, the value of your time spent growing, and the possible hobbyist fee, the expenses involved in growing your own can easily exceed the correlative tax burden of buying marijuana at a licensed store. It's a lot of work and difficult for an amateur to grow anything approaching the quality of that White Widow you bought.

[XV] This is assuming your joint contains around 0.65 grams.

Data from Europe suggests that a legal structure making marijuana easily available from commercial retailers actually decreases the likelihood that users will grow it at home. In 2012, the Netherlands was the only European country with many easily accessible marijuana retailers open to the public. It was also the country with by far the lowest rate of home growing by frequent marijuana users. Just five percent of intensive users in the Netherlands engaged in home growing, whereas in several other countries, including Italy and the Czech Republic, the number was closer to 20 percent.[54] With commercial marijuana reliably available, most users opt for avoiding the hassle of home growing.

This tendency also characterizes home beer brewing. While there aren't solid home brewing statistics from which to draw comparisons, the American Homebrewers Association estimates that roughly one million Americans at least tried to do some home brewing in 2013. The number of Americans who do so with any regularity and produce more than a few gallons is probably much smaller. At most, the number of home brewers amounts to one million out of the roughly 150 million adults who say they drink alcohol.[55] That means less than 1 percent of drinkers even try to brew at home.

Yet, home brewing is much easier than home marijuana cultivation. It takes only a few days to make beer that is ready to drink, while it takes several months to grow and harvest marijuana. A successful batch of beer presents fewer demands than a plant that must be kept healthy. And when a batch of beer goes wrong, relatively little time and capital are wasted, as opposed to the time spent growing marijuana.

As with connoisseur home brewers, the few marijuana home growers grow because they have a passion for the plant. Savings are a secondary consideration, if at all. Most home growers supplement what they can produce at home with store-bought marijuana for variety, quality and convenience.

All considered, while legal marijuana home growing does technically cost the government some potential revenue—just like home beer brewing and growing your own tobacco—the lost revenue represents such a tiny fraction of the overall market that the impact is negligible.

Chapter 6 - Where You Can Smoke

Now that you have left T&R Cannabis with your ounce of bud in its childproof container, the logical question is: Where can you smoke it? To paraphrase President Obama, the point is to inhale.

In New Jersey as with most of the country, the short answer is: almost nowhere. The state prohibits the consumption of marijuana in any public place. This essentially limits you to your home, marijuana smoking lounges, and a few private clubs.

Even while most Americans believe marijuana prohibition was a policy failure and that marijuana should be legal, many look down on using it. Culturally, adults smoking weed are reluctantly tolerated—they are expected to keep it to themselves, and away from kids and others who don't want to take part.

From a public nuisance perspective, the downside of marijuana is that it combines the negative effects of America's two other most common vices, drinking alcohol and smoking cigarettes. Like drinking alcohol, smoking marijuana results in intoxication, and it is a longstanding rule that public spaces are not acceptable places to consume intoxicants or to hang out while intoxicated. And as with tobacco, many people are bothered by the pungent smoke produced by smoking marijuana, especially while eating, since pungent smells from any source interfere with taste. Additionally, the smell of the smoke can easily transfer to clothes and fabrics.

Beyond the cosmetic issues of second hand smoke, there are medical and legal concerns. Smoke of any type can aggravate certain eye conditions and respiratory problems. In addition, the sidestream smoke from marijuana—the smoke that rises from a lit joint or bowl while someone is not inhaling—contains THC. A 1986 study found that it is possible to test positive for detectible levels of cannabinoid metabolites from sidestream smoke if subjected to very long exposure in a poorly ventilated space.[56] This could potentially cause problems for people who, for legal or employment reasons, aren't allowed to consume cannabis—making them fail a drug test even if they have not indulged. Just because marijuana is legal doesn't mean that adults have an inalienable right to use it. Judges can still require adults on probation to remain marijuana-free and to submit to regular tests, just like they can require adults to remain alcohol-free as part of their probation terms. Similarly, some employers refuse to hire people who use marijuana just as some refuse to hire individuals who use tobacco products. In 2007, the world-renowned Cleveland Clinic became one of the first businesses in America to require all applicants to pass a nicotine urine test before being hired.[57]

Because of these considerations, in most places the rules against marijuana smoking are effectively a combination of the rules against public drinking and public cigarette smoking, often extending beyond those restrictions. The vast majority of jurisdictions in the United States have laws prohibiting public marijuana consumption, often called "public joint" laws. For the most part, they are modeled after anti-alcohol open-container laws that prohibit drinking in public. Smoking or consuming marijuana on public property, including streets, sidewalks, and parks, is illegal. In many places it is even illegal to smoke on private property if it is in clear public view, such as on your front lawn.

Marijuana consumption is not only banned in most public and publicly viewable locations, it is also banned in many private businesses. Most localities extended their anti-tobacco smoking laws to cover smoking of any substance, including marijuana. Smoking marijuana in a business, store, or restaurant usually results in fines for the smoker and significant penalties for the company if they knowingly allow people to violate anti-smoking ordinances.

If you try to smoke or openly consume marijuana products while in a park, a restaurant, a store, or walking down the street, you'll probably have your marijuana taken and face a fine ranging from $20-$400 depending on the location. Public consumption is usually a civil infraction, treated like a parking ticket. For particularly egregious (and stupid) offenses, like lighting up in an elementary school while kids are in class, you theoretically could be arrested for a crime such as the contribution to the delinquency of a minor. Fortunately, such stupidity is rare.

Immediately after most states legalized marijuana, the more conservative municipalities within them often instituted large fines for public marijuana consumption to express their displeasure with the new rules. Over the years, even though these places have become more accepting of marijuana use, some of the large penalties remain, thanks to legislative inertia and the money the fines generate—minor citations can be a not-insignificant source of revenue for local police departments. In most places, cops stringently enforce their "public joint" laws if they directly observe it, but it is not something they are actively trying to hunt down. It some ways, it's like anti-littering laws or requirements to pick up your dog's poop. An adult smoking marijuana in public is seen as very inconsiderate, but not a criminal.

Some cities are known for their relaxed attitude. The strictness of enforcement varies not only from place to place, but in some locations, from day to day as well. Just as the police sometimes choose to ignore open container laws during big events like tailgate parties, public marijuana smoking laws are ignored in specific areas during certain marijuana-themed events and celebrations. In municipalities with big outdoor concert venues, there is often an unspoken understanding with the police that they will look the other way. Seattle's annual Hempfest is a classic example. For the three days of the festival, the police department effectively turns a blind eye to the rampant violation of the state's law against smoking marijuana in public. During the first Hempfest post-state legalization, the cops handed out Doritos with information about the new law glued to the bag instead of tickets for violating the law against public smoking.[58] They theoretically could have handled out a lot of tickets.

There are only a few places where it is explicitly legal to smoke marijuana in public, which is the real reason Indica Aficionado chose to build its flagship store in the Oaksterdam District. The rules are different in this special six-block zone of the city. Along with a handful of other towns and cities across the country, Oakland has created these unusual rules for certain areas to boost its tourism industry. The uniquely permissive rules in this special district allow Indica Aficionado to provide some rare perks to its clientele. Even in California, it is illegal to smoke in a business licensed as a retailer, but in Oakland, the Aficionado parent company is allowed to skirt these rules by owning a technically independent marijuana lounge connected to the main store. Their clients are invited to enjoy their purchase in the private lounge or out on the spacious back patio. These unique circumstances make it practical for Indica Aficionado to offer its popular "flight of buds" option. They allow you to select eight different strains to sample, and the store will sell you a very small portion of each. With the purchase, you also get eight specially designed single use paper smoking tubes to preserve the flavor integrity of each choice. Once you purchase your flight, you take it out to the patio to leisurely taste each one while enjoying a complimentary iced tea. Or, you can walk across the street and savor your options in the small park at the center of the district. After you decide which you strains you like the best, you can go back to the store to make a large purchase. This unique experience is what makes the Oaksterdam district a real destination.

The idea for special public cannabis consumption zones to bring in tourism was modeled off of similar rules for alcohol that predated marijuana legalization by decades. At the beginning of the 21st century, the French Quarter in New Orleans, the Las Vegas strip in Nevada, the Power and Light District in Kansas City, Missouri, and the historic district of Savannah, Georgia, were some of the only places in the United States where it was legal to have an open container of alcohol and publicly consume it.[59] Even in these locations, there are still some restrictions—the alcohol usually must be in a plastic container for safety reasons.

Beyond the laws making it illegal to consume marijuana in public, in most states it is also illegal to be intoxicated in public. It is normally a minor offense to be intoxicated in public with any substance, be it alcohol, marijuana, or other drugs. It is even possible to be arrested for public intoxication if you are sober but are merely acting drunk. According to Iowa's intoxication in public law, "A person shall not be intoxicated *or simulate intoxication* in a public place. A person violating this subsection is guilty of a simple misdemeanor."[60] There are a few states, such as Missouri and Nevada, where being drunk in public is not a crime, though.

Public drinking and public smoking are considered minor public nuisances compared with the seriousness of doing so in a car. Just like there are open container laws specifically for vehicles, there are special vehicular anti-marijuana smoking laws. Lit marijuana or even unsealed marijuana anywhere in the passenger compartment of a vehicle can result in fines, points on your license, or even jail time. As of 2010, 39 states had open-container laws that made it illegal to have an open container of alcohol anywhere in the passenger area of a car. A few states still let passengers drink while the vehicle was in motion. At that time, Mississippi was the lone state where a person was not prohibited under state law from drinking alcohol while driving, as long as their blood-alcohol level was below the legal limit.[61] That behavior, though, could get you in trouble under many of the local laws in a state filled with many dry counties.

So, you have returned home to your place in New Jersey after your trip to T&R Cannabis. After struggling with removing that childproof top, you probably expect to be able to sit on your couch and privately enjoy the quality bud you just bought, but you could be wrong. Even in a private residence, there is no guarantee of the right to smoke marijuana. In some states and cities, landlords can ban smoking tobacco and/or marijuana as a condition of the lease. Burning anything can potentially lead to fires, smoke can bother other tenants depending on how the apartment is ventilated, and it normally costs more to clean an apartment where people have smoked. Violating a lease agreement is rarely a crime, but it can result in civil action and possible eviction. For example, in 2011, California passed the Smoke-Free Housing Law giving landlords the explicit right to make their rental properties smoke free. This included not only prohibiting smoking inside, but anywhere on the premises as well.[62]

If you own your home, you should be able to lay back and legally enjoy your purchase in peace. It's also worth remembering that some of these civil issues regarding rent concern only actual smoking. You can still consume your marijuana in other ways, such as sprays, lozenges, extracts, certain vaporizers, etc., which won't damage rental property with smoke.

Cannabis "Coffee Shops" and Marijuana Lounges

The rule of thumb in 99 percent of the country is that an adult can consume marijuana only at home, at a limited number of truly private clubs, or at specially licensed marijuana lounges commonly known as "coffee shops." While "coffee shop" is a strange name for an establishment where people go to smoke weed—and coffee might not even be sold—it is what these places were dubbed in Amsterdam when it was one of the few places on Earth people where could openly buy marijuana, and the name has stuck. When the coffee-shop phenomena started in the Netherlands, marijuana was still technically illegal, so an intentionally ambiguous name was selected. Thanks to tradition, we are stuck with the needlessly confusing nomenclature.

Luckily, New Jersey is among the 22 green states that permit them, and not too far away is Franklin Township, one of few municipalities in the state that didn't adopt zoning rules against them. When faced with a funding crunch, the township decided to take advantage of the potential revenue from taxes and licensing fees on such businesses. Just as there are very different licensing fees and requirements for liquor stores and bars, the same is true for marijuana retail stores and lounges. Even in the states that allow public marijuana lounges, they can be difficult to find in 2030 because of local restrictions. A combination of anti-marijuana opinion, NIMBY (not in my backyard) sentiment, and bars trying to limit competition has ensured that.

The regulations governing the purchase of vodka at liquor stores are very different from the regulations that govern buying a martini at a bar. The same is true with marijuana: There is a legal distinction between marijuana sold for on-premise consumption and marijuana sold for off-premise consumption. Just because it is legal to sell something doesn't necessarily mean it is legal to run a business where people can consume it. While this may seem like a strange principle, it has a long history with alcohol.

In several states, when alcohol prohibition ended and they again allowed the retail sale of booze, they continued to prohibit the on-premise sale of alcoholic drinks. In other words, bars and saloons were kept illegal. Alcohol was tolerated but considered sinful and unfit for public consumption. In some states, on-premise sales were allowed only decades after the end of alcohol prohibition. For instance, the voters of Kansas ended alcohol prohibition in their state in 1948, but their newly-approved amendment clearly stated that open saloons would remain "forever prohibited." It took two decades for the state to relax this restriction, when it approved the Private Clubs Act of 1965, which allowed private clubs to sell alcohol only to official, dues-paying members. True public bars were still illegal. In 1970, the people of Kansas were given the chance to amend the state constitution to allow the public sale of liquor-by-the-drink, but voters narrowly rejected it, 50.8 percent to 49.2 percent. This continued prohibition against open saloons was rigorously enforced. State Attorney General Vern Miller went as far as raiding an Amtrak train in 1972 for selling alcohol while it was traveling through his state. All the alcohol was confiscated from the train's bar, and the conductor, waiter, and bartender were arrested.[63] It wasn't until 1986, over 50 years after the ratification of the 21st Amendment, that voters in Kansas finally repealed the restriction against open saloons. For the first time since 1880 it was finally legal for bars and restaurants to sell liquor-by-the-drink to the general public.[64]

Amazingly, Kansas wasn't even the last state to allow open saloons. Utah, with its large, non-drinking Mormon population, held out even longer. It wasn't until 2009 that the legislature authorized the establishment of true public bars.[65] Up until that point, people were allowed to buy individual drinks only if they were dues-paying members at "private clubs." Before 2009, if you wanted to go out and enjoy a cocktail in a bar-like setting in Utah, you had to fill out an application to become a member and pay a membership fee. By the beginning of the 21st century, these private clubs were functioning almost like public bars just with some ridiculous legal hassles at the door.

This basic pattern was repeated with marijuana legalization. While Colorado and Washington State legalized the off-premise sale of marijuana in 2012, both states still prohibited on-premise sales. Some states didn't legalize public marijuana lounges until years after they first legalized retail marijuana.

One of the three licensed marijuana lounges in Franklin Township, New Jersey, is Jim's Cannabis Coffee Shop. You decide to call up a taxi to take you there, like a responsible, law-abiding adult. Driving while intoxicated on marijuana is as serious an offense as driving while intoxicated on alcohol, and it carries the same penalties. It is true that studies have suggested that driving while high on marijuana is not as dangerous as driving while drunk, but marijuana still causes impairment. Marijuana also doesn't increase risk-taking behavior like alcohol does. Still, these facts can't completely compensate for the impairment THC causes. An analysis published in 2009 in the American Journal on Addiction about marijuana use, driving, and safety found, "This awareness of impairment has behavioral consequences. Several reviews of driving and simulator studies have concluded that marijuana use by drivers is likely to result in decreased speed and fewer attempts to overtake, as well as increased 'following distance.' The opposite is true of alcohol… Not all deficits can be compensated for through the use of behavioral strategies, however. Both alcohol and marijuana use increase reaction time and the number of incorrect responses to emergencies."[66]

Being not nearly *as bad* as alcohol doesn't mean marijuana is objectively not bad when it comes to driving. Driving while high is viewed as taking an unnecessary risk with public safety and is treated harshly. Fortunately, the growing popularity of self-driving cars since 2020 has helped address issues regarding driving while intoxicated.[67] Unfortunately, as you head to the coffee shop, that ounce of quality White Widow you just bought can't come with you. Just like most bars won't let you bring in your own six-pack, Jim's policy is no outside weed.

Jim's Cannabis Coffee Shop started in 2025, but it is situated in an old, renovated bank from the 1930s. While it's a nice building, the main reason it was selected is that it was one of the few spaces on the market at least 1,000 feet away from any school or playground. All the windows are opaque, as required by New Jersey law. Above the door is a vintage-style neon sign featuring the name and what is supposed to be a pot leaf. Below the logo on the front door in bold capital letters, it reads "NO ONE UNDER 21 PERMITTED" and "NO SMOKING OUTSIDE."

Jim's uses the same double door as retail stores and has massive air filters set up to minimize the odor. Once you get past the bouncer and pay the $5 cover, you enter a darkly lit space and are immediately overwhelmed with the smell of good weed. There is a counter to the right, little round tables throughout, and a small stage in the back. The whole place has been decorated with an old-time speakeasy theme to match the 1930s architecture, and the jazz playing in the background completes the effect.

At your table are two menus, the weed menu and the regular menu. What you won't see on either of them is alcohol. It is government policy that the consumption of marijuana with alcohol can be more dangerous that the consumption of either alone, so people are actively discouraged from using them at the same time. Used together, the drugs cause greater impairment and worse decision making than consuming either individually. Studies have shown driving under the influence of alcohol combined with marijuana is more dangerous that driving under the influence of either alone.[68] This is why the FDA prohibits marijuana and alcohol being packaged together, and why almost nowhere in the country can you find an establishment that legally sells both at the same time for on-premise consumption.

The regular menu offers coffee, tea, soda, snacks, and appetizers. The weed menu is where the really interesting stuff is. At Jim's, there are 12 different strains of bud listed, all of them organic. Next to each is its percentage of the major cannabinoids and its price per gram. As with beer prices at a bar compared to a liquor store, the marijuana here is almost three times as expensive as at T&R Cannabis. You are really paying for the whole experience, not just the bud. Each patron is limited to purchasing no more than four grams per visit to prevent excessive consumption and to stop people from using these lounges as de facto retail stores. You are not supposed to take your unconsumed marijuana products with you.

The weed menu also has five different hashes, six different extracts, a plethora of marijuana-infused baked goods all made in house, and several different THC hot chocolate options. Cannabis lounges with their own kitchens are the places where you can legally buy pre-made pot brownies in 2030. The FDA doesn't allow the off-premise sale of marijuana baked goods because they are considered too appealing to minors and too likely to be consumed accidently. Lounges that are closed to minors can get around these restrictions only if they make their own baked goods in the store and don't allow consumers to remove marijuana products from the premises. Jim's specialties are their marijuana baked goods. They are delicious and strong.

In large print, the menu indicates that there is a $5 rental charge for a vaporizer, and at the very bottom, you notice something you probably weren't expecting at a cannabis coffee shop: It says "No Smoking." Only vaporizing weed is allowed. Vaporizers are designed to heat the marijuana to a high enough temperature that the psychoactive components turn into an inhalable vapor without burning the plant material. Studies have shown that vaporizers release the same amount of active ingredients with fewer harmful chemicals.[69] Depending on how the vaporizers are constructed, they also produce significantly less sidestream smoke than a joint, which is important. In 2027,

Franklin Township followed New York City's lead by adopting a vaporizer-only policy for marijuana lounges to protect the health of workers at these establishments.

New York City has often led the nation in adopting so-called "nanny state" regulations to improve public health. In 2002, it adopted one of the earliest bans on cigarette smoking in restaurants and bars. In 2008, it became the first major city in the country to ban trans-fats, and in 2012, it was the first city to pass a law limiting the size of soda that could be sold.[70] New York City reprised this role after the state legalized marijuana in 2022. It became one of the first major places in the country to ban the actual smoking of marijuana in licensed marijuana lounges. It is still legal to consume marijuana in specially licensed coffee shops in the city, but patrons can consume it only using a vaporizer.

While such bans are often opposed by marijuana users and principled libertarians, they have spread rapidly thanks to the overlapping priorities of anti-smoking public health officials and sectors of the marijuana industry. Local politics often makes strange bedfellows.

Anti-smoking officials support such bans for obvious reasons, but in New York City the bans created a surprising financial boon for a certain segment of the marijuana industry. To begin with, such a ban creates a demand for vaporizer manufacturers' products. More importantly, the vaporizer-only rule created another revenue source for coffee shops. The regulation was designed so that most vaporizers fell short of its strict requirements. Vaporizers were required to have redundant safety cutoffs and thermally insulated casings. The ordinance in New York City effectively meant only bulky and rather expensive models could be used—the type people don't normally carry around. This meant patrons needed to rent these vaporizers from coffee shops, an added service that coffee shops could charge for. Are these safety rules really necessary or even logical? No, but if you expect all government regulations to make sense, you haven't been paying attention.

Instead of opposing the spread of vaporizer-only rules, many marijuana lounges remained neutral or privately supported the change. Marijuana lounges lobbied behind the scenes to make sure that if their municipality adopted these rules, the regulations would allow only the bulky vaporizers that patrons would need to rent. This is why you are going to need to shell out another $5 to Jim's Cannabis Coffee Shop before you can enjoy the gram you bought from them.

This is the nature of local marijuana politics in the post-legalization era. The desires of marijuana users normally—but not always—line up with those of the marijuana industry. The marijuana industry's needs rarely line up with the goals of public health officials or those opposed to marijuana, but there are areas where their priorities align. The alcohol and marijuana industries often will be fighting at one moment and working together at the next. Different segments of the marijuana industry will fight over their share of the profits. Once the simple question of whether marijuana should be legal was settled, the low-level political decisions about marijuana evolved into more complicated fights over public health, consumer choice, and simple market advantage. What constitutes an actual "pro-marijuana" or "anti-marijuana" agenda has become a rather fluid concept.

Private Clubs

Unlike in California or New Jersey, if you want to go to a marijuana lounge in North Carolina you are basically out of luck. The problem is that North Carolina is a marijuana control state. Alcohol control states still allow private restaurants and bars to buy alcohol from the government and then sell it for on-premise consumption, and the same is true in some marijuana control states. The problem is that the North Carolina state legislature chose to prohibit this type of business.

Smoking marijuana is banned in all public places in North Carolina, but you can smoke at some of the private clubs in the state that allow it, which is similar to how alcohol was once treated in parts of the country. North Carolina requires that the club be truly private. It can't just be a legal fiction that allows someone to effectively run what is a cannabis coffee shop in all but name. If a club is going to allow marijuana use and/or provide it, the club needs to meet certain criteria. Rules include: New members must be approved by a vote of the members, advertising for club events must be clear the event is for members and invited guests only, visitors can't be invited at the door but instead need a prearranged invitation from a member, etc.[XVI] Deciding what legally differentiates a private club from a public establishment is not just a legal headache in states that don't allow public marijuana lounges, it is a long-standing regulatory issue across the county. In many states, the rules

---

[XVI] These are the rules a private club in Washington State must follow if it wants to sell liquor to its members.
Private Club Handbook. Washington State Liquor Control Board.
https://www.liq.wa.gov/publications/ClubHandbook-092008Update.pdf

governing alcohol sales at private clubs—say, a golf club or an American Legion hall—are significantly different from the rules governing a bar. Similarly, in states that allow marijuana lounges there are special marijuana rules for private clubs.

These special private club rules for marijuana have helped spark a minor revival in some older fraternal organizations like Elk Lodges. This is a fitting example of history repeating itself, since the Benevolent and Protective Order of Elks originally started as a social club over 100 years ago to get around New York City's restrictions on public taverns.

Taken together, the overlapping restrictions on public consumption, public intoxication, and smoking mean that a very limited number of locations technically allow an adult to consume marijuana, even after legalization.

It is important to remember that the vast majority of Americans don't smoke marijuana regularly, and rules in a democracy are written by the majority. Mostly, the laws and regulations have been written so that Americans who choose not to engage in marijuana will rarely be exposed to someone who does. The majority sees marijuana use as a bad habit that should be tolerated but not celebrated. It is something adults should be legally allowed to partake in, but only privately, away from polite society. The enforcement of laws against adult marijuana use in public is not considered a priority, but marijuana users are expected to be considerate and respectful of social conventions. People who violate the laws can expect to be punished.

Chapter 7 – Who Is Smoking

Finally, after you get some bud and find a place to smoke, you might be wondering whom to share it with. There are millions of adults across the country who would be happy to share with you, but they are still only a small minority. Legalization has not turned the country into a nation of potheads.

In a given state in the months directly after legalization, there was a celebratory bump in marijuana usage, but it didn't last long. Former smokers who had not used marijuana in years went out and smoked a few celebratory joints, but for the most part people rather quickly went back to not using or very rarely using marijuana.

For a majority of people both during prohibition and after legalization, the decision to use or not use marijuana had relatively little to do with its legal status. The decision was based mostly on a host of other factors—issues such as personal enjoyment, health, preference, religion, available time, cost, etc.

Skydiving is legal, but very few people choose to try it and even fewer do it regularly. Legal status is far from the primary driving force in decision-making.

The fact is, even before legalization, marijuana was widely available through the black market or the gray medical marijuana market. In many states, thanks to earlier decriminalization, the penalties for personal possession were often minor, and the chances of getting busted for simple possession were small. In some states that approved medical marijuana before full legalization, it was easy for determined people to obtain a physician's recommendation to use marijuana, which for the most part protected the individual from arrest for use or minor possession. Relatively few people were choosing to abstain from marijuana *solely* because it was illegal. In 2010, it was calculated that for the equivalent of every 11,000-12,000 joints consumed, there was just one marijuana arrest.[71] That was hardly a significant legal risk for many regular people.

Morals, personal preference, and social norms guide most people's decisions, not raw legalism or fear of the police. The vast majority of Americans who choose not to steal aren't held back by the fear of being caught and prosecuted—they don't steal because they think stealing is wrong. Americans normally form nice, orderly lines at stores, not because they think the police will arrest them if they don't, but as a result of social norms and a desire to be fair and polite. People are not crazed, stupid animals who are just barely restrained from committing evil acts or self-destructive behavior by the ever-present threat of law enforcement.

The same was true of alcohol use both during the final years and immediately after prohibition ended in the United States. While it is hard to collect accurate statistics about a black market, studies have indicated that the repeal of alcohol prohibition did not cause a huge jump in consumption. Research has found that the level of alcohol consumption in the first several years following the ratification of the 21st Amendment appeared to be about the same as the level of consumption in the last few years of prohibition.[72]

In 2012, the last year before states started legalizing marijuana, roughly 12.1 percent of Americans over the age of 12 had used marijuana in the past year, and 7.3 percent had used it in the last month.[73] That translates to roughly 31.5 million Americans using marijuana with some frequency. In 2030, roughly 15 percent Americans in this same age group had used marijuana in the past year and 9 percent in the last month—a modest overall increase.[XVII]

This slight increase in use was due to factors that were independent of marijuana's change in legal status. One important element was the demographic shift. Very few Americans born before 1950 ever tried marijuana when they were young, while a significant percentage of adults born after that year did. The older generation grew up with extreme anti-marijuana propaganda and stuck to their habits of abstaining from marijuana throughout their lives. Once this generation was fully replaced, overall rates rose. Another factor was a change in social opinions about marijuana. People in all age groups started

---

[XVII] This is my own personal estimate, which I believe is reasonable based on the data I lay out in this chapter.

to view using it as safer and less immoral. In 2006, Pew found 50 percent of Americans considered smoking marijuana morally wrong. By 2013 that number had dropped to only 32 percent.[74] This social trend was not an effect of legalization—it was one of its causes.

The change in legal status was, in some indirect ways, partly responsible for increased use. It reduced prices, but high excise taxes helped to lessen this impact. Legalization did make marijuana more convenient for adults to purchase. It also removed some concerns such as employer drug testing. Finally, it made it easier and more likely that Americans would use marijuana for medical reasons.

During the multiple political battles that took place to finally end marijuana prohibition, opponents often tried to scare voters with claims about soaring usage after legalization. Their claims were never grounded in firm, real-world data. Even back at the beginning of the 21st century, it was clear that there was little if any correlation between use, legal status, and level of penalties.

Usage Before and After Decriminalization and Adoption of Medical Marijuana

Multiple studies that examined overall marijuana usage in a particular region before and after marijuana rules were changed found that they had little to no impact on the number of people using the drug. Individual American and Australian states proved ideal testing grounds for trying to isolate the impact, if any, of reducing penalties for marijuana consumption. Comparing states that adopted reform with their neighbors gave solid insight into which behavioral changes were caused by the law, and which were part of broader national trends.

A 1995 study in the Australian Journal of Public Health looked at the usage rates in Australia comparing different regions that did and did not decriminalize the use of marijuana in the late 1980s. The study showed that "although the NCADA survey data indicate that there were increases in cannabis use in South Australia in 1985-1993, they cannot be attributed to the effects of partial decriminalisation, because similar increases occurred in other states."[75]

The same general pattern was found in American states. In 1997, the Connecticut Law Revision Commission looked at studies on the impact of marijuana decriminalization. It found that reduced penalties were not responsible for increased usage:[76]

"Studies of states that have reduced penalties for possession of small amounts of marijuana have found that (1) expenses for arrests and prosecution of marijuana possession offenses were significantly reduced, (2) any increase in the use of marijuana in those states was less than increased use in those states that did not decrease their penalties and "the largest proportionate increase occurred in those states with the most severe penalties", and (3) reducing the penalties for marijuana has virtually no effect on either the choice or frequency of use of alcohol or illegal "harder" drugs such as cocaine."

Similarly, the adoption of medical marijuana laws in certain states did not cause a noticeable change in usage compared to other states. This provides an even better example, because the relaxed nature of the medical marijuana systems in some states was almost de facto legalization. A 2011 study in the

Annals of Epidemiology analyzed marijuana use in states before and after medical marijuana laws were approved, compared to other states in the same time period. It found that "once we control for any unmeasured state characteristics that do not change over time, we find very little evidence that passing MMLs increases reported use, among adolescents or any other age group... Our difference-in-differences estimates suggest little detectable effects of passing MMLs on marijuana use or perceived riskiness of use among adolescents or adults, which is consistent with some limited prior evidence on arrestees and emergency department patients."[77]

International Comparisons

A quick look at international data comparing usage to the severity of a nation's laws regarding marijuana should have made it clear to anyone that there is little to no causal relationship. The best proof that marijuana legalization alone was not going to turn our country into a nation of stoners was in the Netherlands. In 1976, marijuana was effectively legalized in Holland, and by the early 1980s the government started tolerating the emergence of coffee shops that openly sold marijuana. By the 1990s, there were hundreds of these quasi-legal coffee shops all over the country, and the government started taking a more active role in licensing them. Aspects of the Dutch marijuana industry still exist in a legal gray area, in part because of international treaties. The bottom line, however, is that for the people of the Netherlands at the beginning of the 21st century, marijuana was incredibly easy to buy at hundreds of licensed retail outlets, and it had been that way for decades.

This made the country rather uniquely tolerant of cannabis and a perfect test case for the long-term impact of legalization.

Despite this long history of tolerance, the Netherlands did not have the highest marijuana usage rates in the world or even in Europe. According to the United Nations Office on Drugs and Crime 2013 World Drug Report, multiple countries had much higher rates of marijuana use than the Netherlands at that time. The annual prevalence of use among people age 15-64 was noticeably higher in Australia, Canada, the Czech Republic, France, Italy, Israel, New Zealand, Poland, Spain, and the United States.[78]

Comparing the United States to the rest of the industrialized world shows what a complete failure its aggressive war on marijuana was at stopping people from using cannabis. Despite having some of the tougher marijuana laws and aggressive enforcement, America in the early 21st century had one of the highest usage rates in the world. In 2010, the United States had an annual prevalence of use almost twice as high as the Netherlands.

In their 2011 annual report looking at a decade of usage data across multiple European countries, the European Monitoring Centre for Drugs and Drug Addiction wrote, "the legal impact hypothesis, in its simplest form, states that a change in the law will lead to a change in prevalence, with increased penalties leading to a fall in drug use and reduced penalties to a rise in drug use... However, in this 10-year period, for the countries in question, no simple association can be observed between legal changes and cannabis use prevalence."[79]

Steps Taken to Reduce Use After Legalization

It is theoretically possible that we would have seen a large increase in marijuana use if it had been completely legalized without any controls, taxes, or restrictions, but no one seriously made the case for that. Even the main organizations that campaigned for marijuana legalization thought it should be regulated and taxed.

Decades of experience with tobacco regulation proved that the blunt hatchet of prohibition is not the only tool the government has to discourage certain behaviors. According to the CDC in 1970, the year the United States Congress passed the Public Health Cigarette Smoking Act banning the advertising of cigarettes on television and radio, 37.4 percent of adults smoked cigarettes. Thanks to in part to restrictions on advertising, public education efforts, and increased excise taxes, cigarette use fell slowly but steadily for the next 40 years. By 2010, only 19.3 percent of American adults smoked cigarettes.[80] The success of anti-smoking campaigns from 1970-2010 showed that reducing the use of a legal drug doesn't require a "war" mentality. The example of tobacco also shows that concerns that marijuana legalization would "send the wrong message" were unfounded. Even if the government allows something to be legal, it can still easily send the message that it considers it a bad idea.

Following the legalization of marijuana, basically every government mechanism used to discourage the use of alcohol or cigarettes was applied to marijuana. When regulations regarding alcohol and cigarettes diverged—for example, the respective legal minimum ages of 21 and 18—the government applied the tougher one to the newly legalized cannabis.

As discussed earlier in the book, excise taxes and licensing fees were used to artificially inflate the price. Strict bans were placed on advertising. Warning labels were made mandatory. Anything that could make marijuana products seem appealing to children—for instance, ads featuring cartoons or candy flavoring—were prohibited. A portion of the tax revenue from marijuana was also set aside to pay for drug treatment and public service announcements. Only face-to-face purchases in secured locations were allowed, as cannabis deliveries and marijuana ordered over the Internet were considered too likely to end up in the hands of minors.

Public health experts and concerned parents weren't the only ones pushing for these restrictions. The alcohol industry encouraged the government to make all new marijuana regulations at least as restrictive as those in place for alcohol, so that marijuana wouldn't have a regulatory edge. This is a large part of the reason the minimum legal age for recreational marijuana is 21.

There is no particularly logical reason it should be 21 as opposed to 18, 20, or 25, but the consensus was that the age limit for marijuana use in the United State should be same as that for alcohol. Almost all of the states that had approved of marijuana legalization prior to the federal government ending its prohibition had selected a minimum age of 21. This was the age set by Amendment 64 in Colorado and Initiative 502 in Washington State. When Congress approved the Regulation and Control of Cannabis Act of 2022, it followed suit. Having an age limit on par with alcohol also helped reduce opposition from the alcohol lobby, which could have been significant.

Youth Usage

The tough age restriction put on legal marijuana hasn't completely stopped teens from using it, just as the age restrictions on tobacco and alcohol haven't been 100 percent effective. Teen marijuana use is still fairly common—it is tough to stop determined teenagers. Of course, prohibition did an even worse job of keeping marijuana away from minors. Despite marijuana being completely illegal for everyone from 2006-2009, more American teens said it was easier for them to get marijuana than beer. In 2012, significantly more high school students said they had tried marijuana than had tried tobacco even though any 18-year-old can buy cigarettes with ease.[81]

The fact that an illegal substance was easily accessible by minors should not be surprising. During marijuana prohibition, marijuana was completely controlled by the black market, and sellers had no reason to check ID or care about age. If anything, black market illegal dealers openly welcomed the business of minors. At T&R Cannabis, anyone under 21 is turned away before they can even enter the store. When states starting legalizing medical marijuana it did not increase use among teens in the first several years. In fact, indicators are that the legalization of medical marijuana may have been slightly associated with reduced use among minors.[82]

Chapter 8 – Impact on Public Health

If you're an adult who chooses to indulge in marijuana, its legalization has been important to you: It's made cannabis cheaper, more convenient, of higher quality, and safer.

If you're an adult who has no interest in cannabis, its legalization has had surprisingly little direct impact on your life. Thanks to restrictions on advertising, store locations, and public smoking, most non-users rarely ever actually see a marijuana business or people using it. The tax revenue from marijuana and the law enforcement savings has probably made some real improvements to your life, but the direct connection isn't obvious at first glance. The excise taxes probably allowed for the construction of a new park, a slight reduction in your property taxes, and a few extra teachers at your public school. Since most government revenue goes into the same general fund, it is tough to pinpoint what would and wouldn't have been paid for without marijuana tax revenue. While not huge compared to the overall size of government, this new revenue comes to several billion dollars a year.[XVIII]

One aspect of legalization that does concern everyone is its impact on public health—the well-being of our neighbors, family, and friends touches us not only on a personal level, but impacts the entire country financially as well. Health care programs such as Medicare and Medicaid are some of the largest items on both federal and state budgets.

It is important to distinguish between the public health impact of marijuana legalization and the public health impact of all marijuana use. After all, marijuana prohibition failed miserably in its goal of stopping people from smoking weed. Millions of Americans were using marijuana when it was illegal, and millions of Americans would still be smoking in 2030 whether or not there had been a change in the law. The limited public health problems associated with people using this plant still existed during prohibition. Prohibition didn't stop people from using marijuana; it just made it more dangerous.

Legalization really only did two things that made a real impact on public health. First, it slightly increased the number of people who use weed and the amount being consumed, because marijuana was cheaper and slightly easier to get.

[XVIII] A 2010 White Paper from the CATO institute estimated that marijuana legalization would save the federal and local governments around $8.7 billion a year and also generate about that same amount in revenue.
Miron, Jeffery A. and Waldock, Katherine. The Budgetary Impact of Ending Drug Prohibition. CATO Institute. 2010
http://www.cato.org/publications/white-paper/budgetary-impact-ending-drug-prohibition

Second, it dramatically improved the safety of almost all the marijuana that was going to be consumed anyway.

The Risk of Marijuana Use

The public health concerns associated with marijuana use are relatively minor. Smoking marijuana does tend to elevate an individual's heart rate immediately afterwards. This can be an issue for people with serious heart problems, who should be advised against using marijuana due to the increased risk of having a heart attack. By comparison, the risk seems to be on par with that of having sex or exercising.[83] (Of course, no one thinks that's a justification for making sex illegal.)

Studies have indicated that THC might moderately reduce male fertility.[84] Obviously, marijuana has not turned out to be an effective birth control method, given that plenty of regular users have children, but it is advisable to avoid it while trying to get pregnant if you already have a low sperm count. Also, marijuana intoxication impairs short-term memory and can cause anxiety. It is not advised for people with certain mental health issues or those about to engage in tasks that require focus, e.g. studying.

Marijuana smoke does contain many of the same carcinogens and irritants found in tobacco smoke, but even heavy marijuana users tend to consume only a fraction of the amount of material that a regular cigarette smoker does. Some studies have indicated long-term marijuana smoking is associated with respiratory complications, including increased cough and wheezing,[85] but there seems to be no or very little association between marijuana smoking and lung/throat cancers.

A study in Cancer Epidemiology, Biomarker & Prevention concluded, "A major limitation of previous studies was the relative lack of subjects with use >10 joint-years, which limited their power to detect effects. In contrast, we had ample numbers of such users for oral and lung cancers. Nonetheless, and contrary to our expectations, we found no positive associations between marijuana use and lung or [upper aerodigestive tract] cancers. Although we observed positive dose-response relations of marijuana use to oral and laryngeal cancers in the crude analyses, the trend was no longer observed when adjusting for potential confounders, especially cigarette smoking."[86]

Cannabis can be habit forming and some individuals can become what is classified as clinically dependent, but it is less "addictive" than most other common drugs. About 9 percent of people who try marijuana are said to become dependent. By comparison, the figure is 15 percent for alcohol, 17 percent for cocaine, and an incredible 32 percent for nicotine.[87] People are not only less likely to become dependent on marijuana, but being dependent on marijuana is far less problematic than being dependent on most other drugs because of its relative safety.

Marijuana does cause intoxication. This can result in bad decision-making, and it should be avoided while operating heavy equipment. Marijuana intoxication is not, though, associated with increased incidence of violence and injury. Unlike other drugs like alcohol, which cause excessive risk-taking, marijuana tends to make individuals more cautious. People on marijuana tend to overcompensate for physical impairment. Several studies found an increased likelihood of injury right after drinking or using some other drugs, but a decreased likelihood of being injured after consuming marijuana. People who are high might even be less likely to injure themselves than people who are sober. One study concluded, "The results of our study corroborate research showing the detrimental effect of alcohol use on injury. The results for cannabis use were quite surprising, as they were associated with less risk of injury."[88] Marijuana use is also not associated with violence. A 1993 National Academy of Science research review found that, "The majority of the evidence in experimental studies with animals and humans, as well as most data from chronic users, emphasizes that cannabis preparations (e.g., marihuana, hashish) or THC decrease aggressive and violent behavior."[89] The stereotypical image of stoners being laid back actually has a kernel of truth—unlike the absurd image of marijuana turning teens into crazed killers put forward by Anslinger and his ilk decades ago.

A theoretical lethal dose of marijuana for an adult is so large that it is nearly physically impossible to consume that much. Animal studies suggest that the lethal dose for an adult male would probably be around 100 grams of pure THC—or well over a thousand times a normal dose. FDA data from 1997 to 2005 shows there wasn't a single case in that timeframe in which marijuana was the primary suspected cause of death.[90] By comparison, in 2008 alone, drug overdoses caused 36,450 deaths in the United States. Of those, 20,044 were from prescription medications with three-fourths of prescription overdoses caused by opioid pain relievers.[91]

In relative terms, marijuana is remarkably safe. It is not strongly associated with an increased risk of injury, cancer, or overdose. The same can't be said for tobacco, alcohol, and many prescription drugs. Given these facts, the slight increase in marijuana use caused by legalization may have even been a small net positive from a public health perspective. Some of the increase in cannabis use represents people choosing to smoke marijuana instead of drinking heavily,[XIX] and others using marijuana products for pain relief instead of opioid pain relievers. Marijuana is arguably much safer than either.

Purity and Safety

While the increase in marijuana use caused by legalization is probably at best a mixed bag for public health, in terms of the overall safety of marijuana use, it's been a clear positive. Since millions of Americans were going to consume marijuana anyway, the heavily regulated legal market ensured that it would be as safe as possible. Almost all marijuana consumed in the country in 2030 is repeatedly tested for dangerous contaminants, chemicals, and pathogens. The origin label requirements of seed-to-sale systems also mean that if there is a problem, government regulators can easily track it back to the cause, issue a recall, and potentially shut down the operation responsible.

Aside from direct regulation, the nature of a legitimate market helps keep a product safe in ways a black market never

---

[XIX] Research indicates that the "legalization of marijuana for medical purposes has been associated with reductions in heavy drinking, especially among 18- to 29-year-olds, and with an almost 5 percent decrease in beer sales."
Editorial Board. New York Times. Nov 3, 2013.
http://www.nytimes.com/2013/11/04/opinion/marijuana-and-alcohol.html?_r=0

could. The inherent incentives for safety are completely different. In a legitimate market, brand carries significant value. A company has a lot invested in maintaining the image of its brand, since that brand can attain familiarity and cultural prevalence. Companies have a huge incentive to guard the integrity of their brand by producing a clean product. In a black market, a seller can't legally trademark a brand, and he is always one big bust away from being out of business. As a result, he doesn't have the same long-term focus.

Finally, the legal market gives consumers access to the court system. A producer that is not making a safe product or that falsely advertises has to worry about being sued for negligence. In the black market, there were no authorities to turn to, nor a court system for the redress of grievances. People don't normally go to the police and admit they have committed a crime just so they can pursue a class action lawsuit against a drug dealer. The stringent regulations and market forces that attended legalization helped guarantee marijuana was not tainted, deliberately or accidentally. Just as the end of alcohol prohibition resulted in the improved safety of alcohol, so too did the end of marijuana prohibition improve the safety of marijuana used by adults.

During alcohol prohibition, the clandestine nature of the product resulted in unscrupulous dealers knowingly and unknowingly selling Americans unsafe liquor. Illegal stills would often use tools and materials that were inappropriate for the distillation of alcohol, such as old car radiators. Unsafe stills could leak dangerous chemicals into the liquor, including glycol and lead. The liquor could end up being stored or shipped in containers that would leak unhealthy chemicals into the product, or the dealer could have added toxic chemicals to try to enhance the taste.

One of the most outrageous negative consequences of alcohol prohibition was the effort by the United States government to indirectly poison its own citizens. Even though the production of alcohol for drinking was banned, ethanol was and still is an extremely important industrial product used by a whole host of industries. As early as 1906, ingredients were added to industrial ethanol to "denature" it, making it unpleasant to drink. This was sufficient to stop most people from drinking industrial components until prohibition created a black market demand for any alcohol.

The government realized some people were diverting industrial ethanol for human consumption, so it ordered industrial ethanol to be heavily poisoned to try to stop the practice. However, this did not stop unscrupulous criminals and unknowing individuals from using industrial ethanol for drinking. Criminals even found ways to remove some of the chemicals added to make the industrial ethanol fit for drinking, which in turn led the government to engage in what was essentially a chemical arms race, demanding that chemical companies start using more poison. This resulted in the estimated death of at least 10,000 Americans who consumed alcohol that the government made more dangerous, not safer.[92]

A similar problem with tainted goods existed—but to a lesser degree—during marijuana prohibition. Unlike other illicit drugs such as heroin, cocaine or ecstasy, which were sold in a powder or pill form and routinely cut with other substances, sometimes very dangerous ones, black-market marijuana in the United States was normally sold as a raw plant material. This made it easier for people to visually inspect it for obvious issues. While this helped make instances of dangerously tainted marijuana rare during marijuana prohibition, they still occurred. In some instances, marijuana was laced with other, more dangerous drugs. When dealers did this, they would normally advertise the fact, but it still left open the possibility that people could unknowingly consume a far more dangerous drug than they thought they would be.

There were also incidents of marijuana being laced with very dangerous substances to improve its appearance or artificially increase its weight. For example, in 2007, several people in the Leipzig area of Germany were admitted to the hospital due to acute lead poisoning. The source of the problem was determined to be tainted marijuana being sold illegally. It is likely that the presence of lead was the result of a deliberate move by illegal dealers to increase the weight of the marijuana so they could sell it for a greater profit. Lead is cheap and one of the densest materials on earth. By adding a just a small amount lead, the weight of the marijuana was increased by roughly 10 percent. That small increase could translate to increased profit. All told, 95 people required treatment as a result of this incident.[93]

A similar problem occurred in the United Kingdom starting in 2006. There many reports of marijuana adulterated with extremely small glass beads. It was assumed that the glass was added to artificially increase the weight of the cannabis, to increase the price. Inhaling tiny particles of glass is obviously not a great idea for your lungs.[94]

Perhaps more worrying than the rare cases of marijuana purposely being laced with dangerous additives to increase the weight was the general lack of basic safety regulation in the black market. Without regular safety inspections, illegal marijuana would often accidentally be contaminated. Marijuana was sometimes treated with pesticides or herbicides not meant for human consumption or in dosages exceeding acceptable levels. A drug cartel trying to avoid the DEA is not likely to worry about following FDA regulations regarding safe handling of agricultural products. Additionally, at least some marijuana was probably shipped and stored in ways that exposed it to unhealthy chemicals or microbes. Poorly ventilated, clandestine indoor growing operations could result in the growth of mold or bacteria that would contaminate the cannabis. Steep Hills started in 2008 as a private lab created to test medical marijuana in California. It claimed that in its first years, it found roughly 3 percent of the samples sent to them contained unsafe levels of mold.[95] At the time, there was no requirement to have marijuana tested, so it is likely only the most professional and conscientious medical marijuana operations bothered to take part in this independent testing in the first place.

Contaminants can have serious consequences, including death. There was at least one incident of an individual dying from a pathogen potentially contracted from tainted marijuana. A 34-year-old male with a compromised immune system was killed by an infection of Aspergillus fumigatus. The same mold was also found on the marijuana he had been smoking before developing the infection.[96] This was not the only known case of illegal marijuana serving as a vector for infection. Like any other agricultural product, if marijuana is not handled appropriately, it can become a vehicle for foodborne pathogens. The Centers for Disease Control determined that the source of a 1981 outbreak of Salmonella was contaminated marijuana.[97]

While such dangerous incidents were probably rare, we will never know with certainty the extent of the problem. The fact that marijuana was illegal likely kept many people from reporting problems and encouraged them to lie about their habits when being treated for health issues. The black market kept no safety records or systems by which consumers could file complaints.

The criminalization of marijuana also drove people to seek out untested alternatives that often turned out to be more dangerous. One significant example is the spread of "fake weed" at beginning of the 21st century. Companies started selling legal "incense" treated with chemicals such as JWH-018. These were new, artificial cannabinoids created in a lab that mimic the effects of THC. These new chemicals were completely untested from a safety perspective and objectively described by users as not nearly as pleasant an experience as natural marijuana. They may have even been linked to several deaths.[98] The only advantage they had over marijuana was that, until the government eventually took action, they were technically legal, but that was enough to make them fairly popular. For a while, as one chemical was banned, a new, slightly altered, untested version would hit the market. This would not have happened if marijuana were legal at the time.

Keeping People Away From Criminals

Another public health benefit of legalization is that it gives people an alternative to criminals as a source for marijuana. Not only are black market dealers less concerned about quality control, but they are also more commonly engaged in a range of dangerous activities. You hear of people trying to rob liquor stores, but you never hear about people being robbed at gunpoint by their liquor store. This is a real problem with illegal dealers, though.

Additionally, licensed, regulated businesses have a strong motive for not selling you other illegal drugs, but black market dealers have the opposite incentive. The Stevenson brothers would never even think of selling anyone heroin at their T&R Cannabis store and will quickly call the police on any potential illegal dealer if they ever saw one nearby. If even a single incident of an employee trying to sell heroin was reported, it could result in them losing their license, having the entire store seized and bank accounts frozen, and a possible arrest.

During marijuana prohibition, illegal dealers didn't have these concerns. A large dealer would get arrested regardless if they were selling just marijuana or marijuana and heroin. They might as well sell both. By actively pushing cocaine or other drugs on their costumers, they increased the total volume of contraband they sold and maximized their profits.

The only extent to which marijuana was ever a "gateway drug" was that its prohibition made it more likely that an individual using marijuana would need to interact with criminals who would actively try to sell them harder drugs. The de facto legalization of marijuana in the Netherlands broke this connection. A 2013 report for the European Commission found that "Excluding the Netherlands, between 26% (Czech Republic) and 52% (Sweden) of the cannabis users indicate that other drugs are available at the location where they usually buy cannabis. The relatively low proportion in the Netherlands (14% overall, 9% for those who buy in coffee shops) is likely to reflect the policy of separation of the cannabis and hard drugs markets."[99] Full legalization with proper regulation is even more successful at creating this separation. At the time, the Netherlands tolerated the sale of small amounts of marijuana but not commercial growth. This odd legal dynamic meant that coffee shops still needlessly had some connection to a black market.

You can't stop people from using marijuana by making it illegal. The United States tried for decades, and it failed spectacularly. So, if you accept that people are going to use marijuana, you want them to use the safest version possible. A well regulated legal marketplace ensures this, while by comparison, prohibition produces the exact opposite effect.

Chapter 9 – What Becomes of Medical Marijuana

You can't talk about legalization's full impact on public health without also discussing the positive effects it's had for people using marijuana and marijuana-derived drugs for legitimate medical reasons.

At the end of the 20th century, many prohibitionists considered medical marijuana a sham that served only as a back door for legalized pot. While it is true that some activists used state medical marijuana laws to push for complete legalization, and some states' lax rules regulating medical marijuana allowed almost anyone to get a doctor's recommendation for it no matter how minor their medical issue, almost no one in the reform community ever doubted that marijuana has many clear medicinal benefits.

Marijuana has probably been used as a medicine for 5,000 years, if not longer. According to Chinese tradition, Emperor

Shen Nung discovered its medicinal power around 2,700 B.C. For thousands of years, the use of cannabis as medicine was widely documented by both traditional Chinese and Western sources. The famous Roman historian Pliny the Elder wrote about medical uses for the plant roughly 2,000 years ago. A Chinese pharmacopoeia, also dating from around the first century, recommended the plant to treat a wide range of ailments from gout to rheumatism.[100]

Marijuana was medicine for thousands of years before English colonists first arrived in North America, and it was commonly used medicine throughout the United States' early history. Even after the U.S. officially made marijuana illegal, many Americans continued to use it clandestinely for medical purposes, and now that this misguided prohibition has ended, Americans continue to use it for the same reasons.

Modern studies have shown that marijuana and/or its extracts can be an effective treatment for a wide range of ailments. It is a proven appetite stimulant and a very effective anti-nausea agent. Both properties are very important for people undergoing chemotherapy or suffering from AIDS. Marijuana can relieve eye pressure associated with glaucoma. It has also been shown in a double-blind study to be effective in treating Crohn's disease, an inflammatory bowel disease.[101] Many studies have found evidence that cannabis is useful in pain management[102] and can improve quality of life for people suffering from Multiple Sclerosis.[103]

An added benefit of marijuana's medical application is that it has a remarkably low toxicity. Unlike many prescription drugs, there is no risk of overdose with marijuana, and there are relatively few negative side effects. This is particularly important for pain management, since opioid painkillers are more addictive and relatively easy to overdose on.

Its widespread use for medical reasons helped demonstrate that marijuana is safe and can be sold legally with little negative impact on society. Medical marijuana also exposed many older people to the plant, which helped demystify it. Separate from the legal treatment of the term, medical marijuana is and as always has been very real. The actual medical use of marijuana and marijuana derivatives increased noticeably after prohibition was ended.

Neither federal prohibition nor federal legalization changed the fact that marijuana can be effective medicine. If people used it for legitimate medical reasons while it was illegal, it was still *medical marijuana*, even when the government refused to acknowledge the fact or allow its use. The law only changed how people accessed it and how it could be studied. Legalization's effect on "medical marijuana," therefore, has to do with how the concept was legally treated.

The legal impact came in three distinct parts:

1. The unofficial use of recreational marijuana as medicine.

2. FDA-approved medication derived from marijuana.

3. What remains of states' medical marijuana laws and systems after full legalization.

The Unofficial Medical Use of Recreational Marijuana

Just because something is not sold as medicine doesn't mean people can't use it for medical reasons. A person may buy coconut oil for cooking or use it topically to treat dry skin. You can use ginger to make stir-fry or to help with your nausea. One person may drink chamomile tea to enjoy the flavor while another drinks it to help with insomnia. The same is true of "recreational" marijuana.

If you recall, back at T&R Cannabis there are a few strains of high-CBD bud. There are also several marijuana-containing products that are formulated with dosages of THC that would not be of interest for a recreational user. One such product is Jane's Smooth Sailing, a low-dose marijuana extract spray with a label that strongly hints at cannabis' effectiveness in treating motion sickness. Products like this one are sold almost exclusively for medical reasons but can't be explicitly marketed that way. If you ask one of the Stevenson brothers, they will happily expound upon the health benefits of marijuana products with different balances of cannabinoids, but none of the products they'll tell you about make any explicit medical claims. A significant proportion of people who use marijuana for medical reasons simply buy it from recreational stores and repurpose it. Some doctors will even recommend this option. People who buy these products often do so because they prefer "natural" remedies, or depending on their insurance's prescription drug plan, this option saves them money. The strict controls on the labeling and handling of recreational marijuana ensure the safety and consistency of these products. These rules mean that your recreational marijuana was likely subjected to more safety testing than your food, beauty products, and over-the-counter drugs. Many "recreational" marijuana retailers are known for having a large selection of medically oriented marijuana products.

The regulation of these medically focused marijuana strains and products that are not officially classified as medical drugs has been a major cause of contention since Congress approved the Regulation and Control of Cannabis Act. On one side are the established marijuana and the herbal supplement industries, which mainly see this as just another front in their fights with the FDA over similar issues. On the other side is the pharmaceutical lobby. In 2023, the FDA decided to treat marijuana in much the same way it treated herbal supplements when it came to health claims, which many regarded as a real win for the marijuana industry. The FDA tolerates marijuana products that allude to their medical properties, but they're prohibited from making direct claims about their capacity to treat any medical issue.

Herbal supplements are widely used in the United States but are regulated differently by the FDA than pharmaceutical drugs. The FDA demands only that the supplements are not dangerous, not that they are actually proven to work. As a result, the FDA is very strict about the claims herbal supplements can make on their packaging or in their marketing campaigns. An herbal supplement or food product can't claim that it is intended for the prevention, mitigation, or treatment of disease. Only drugs can do that. For example, cranberry pills sold as an herbal supplement can state on the label that they're used for "maintaining the health of the urinary tract," but if the package claims they are for "treating urinary tract infections," it would officially be considered a drug by the FDA and required to meet a much different standard.[104] In 2009, the FDA even warned General Mills that if they didn't change the health claims on their Cheerios package, the agency would classify the cereal as an unapproved drug, forcing it to be removed from store shelves. The offending language on package stated, "you can Lower Your Cholesterol 4% in 6 weeks" and "Did you know that in just 6 weeks Cheerios can reduce bad cholesterol by an average of 4 percent?" The FDA deemed that these claims crossed the line by implying the cereal could mitigate a medical condition.[105]

Marijuana as Official FDA-Approved Medicine

Even after the federal government legalized marijuana, the FDA never approved the raw, unprocessed plant material as a medical drug, especially if it was meant to be smoked. The FDA simply doesn't treat raw plants or herbs this way, since a raw plant material can't meet the high level of standardization the FDA requires for a prescription drug. When it comes to naturally occurring remedies, the FDA approves only individual chemicals or a limited combination of chemicals that can be isolated from these natural sources as medication. The FDA has a heavy bias toward single chemicals, though the agency has on a few occasions approved botanical prescription drugs that are derived from plant material, with varying degrees of purification to standardize the active ingredients. This is extremely rare, though. By early 2013, only two botanical drugs had been approved as prescription medication by the FDA.[106] The first was sinecatechins, a topical green tea extract, and the second was crofelemer, an anti-diarrheal drug derived from a South American tree.

The relaxation of the laws around marijuana did, however, make conducting FDA-approved research on the medical benefits of cannabis dramatically easier. During marijuana prohibition, medical research on cannabis was trapped in a Kafkaesque bureaucratic nightmare. For decades, the federal government classified marijuana as a Schedule I drug, meaning it had "no currently accepted medical use in treatment in the United States."[XX] In part, this designation was used to justify giving the National Institute on Drug Abuse a monopoly over all marijuana products in the country that could be used in research approved by the federal government. In effect, the NIDA used this power to deny access to researchers testing whether marijuana could be an effective treatment for medical conditions. In 2011, the NIDA went as far as denying researchers access to government-approved cannabis for trial to determine its impact on post-traumatic stress disorder, even though the trial's protocols were already approved by the FDA.[107] Of course, NIDA's blockage of an already-approved supply for research means there were no FDA-approved studies proving marijuana had medical benefits. This gave the DEA its justification for keeping marijuana Schedule I and a reason for keeping the control over the supply of research marijuana solely in the hands of the NIDA. In turn, the NIDA could continue to block any FDA-approved research, keeping the cycle going.

[XX]As of the publishing of this book in 2013, marijuana is still listed as schedule I.

During these dark ages for marijuana research, the only drug based on marijuana that was approved by the FDA was Dronabinol, a synthetic version of THC. It was first approved as a medical treatment in 1985. It was not overwhelmingly popular, nor did it obviate the need for medical marijuana. Pure THC lacks many of medical marijuana's benefits, because it is missing the other cannabinoids that moderate its effects and add other benefits. The fact that the government approved this drug during the height of prohibition only highlighted the bizarreness of the legal situation: The government was simultaneously saying marijuana had no medical value and that its main active ingredient has proven medical value.

Legalization ended this absurd catch-22. Finally, scientists could conduct government-approved research around all aspects of cannabis, and drug companies could develop new prescription drugs based on marijuana. This resulted in prescription drugs that are based on naturally occurring cannabinoids normally found in very small concentrations and other drugs that are new, chemical variations of natural cannabinoids. Some prescription drugs consist of broad-spectrum extracts of marijuana's main active ingredients, which very closely resemble the effect of marijuana. They come as pills, sprays, or inhalers. These prescription marijuana extracts happen to be remarkably similar to several products on the recreational market, which has resulted in some legal disputes.

Approved medicines like these are the main way in which people with legitimate medical problems get "medical marijuana" in the year 2030. Some of these drugs based on natural cannabinoids are more acutely targeted than marijuana proper, so they have fewer side effects. A prescription broad-spectrum cannabis extract has certain benefits over buying a similar recreational product, such as Jane's Smooth Sailing Spray—financially, your insurance might cover the cost of a prescription, and these medications are not subject to the same excise taxes as recreational marijuana. Prescription drugs can also be given to minors and are allowed in employment settings that prohibit the use of recreational marijuana.

What Became of States' Old Medical Marijuana Laws

Some states legalized medical marijuana and developed fairly large medical marijuana systems years before they legalized recreational marijuana. For a while after prohibition ended, the medical marijuana systems in these states ran in parallel to their recreational systems. For example, both Washington State's Initiative 502 and Colorado's Amendment 64 explicitly stated these new recreational laws would not change the medical marijuana laws in the state.

While these dual systems coexisted, participating in medical marijuana programs sometimes had certain advantages. Initiative 502 limited regular Washingtonians to an ounce of marijuana, and it was still illegal to grow it at home for personal use. But when recreational marijuana was legalized, qualified medical marijuana patients in the state could grow up to 15 plants and could possess up to 24 ounces.[108] In the early days after Amendment 64 passed in Colorado, you needed to be 21 to buy recreational marijuana, but only 18 to buy medical marijuana. Medical marijuana dispensaries also faced different local regulations. Some municipalities banned recreational marijuana businesses but not medical ones.

Eventually, these state governments tried to unify these parallel systems. In some cases, the restrictions on recreational marijuana were loosened to mirror those on medical marijuana, while in others the restrictions on medical marijuana were tightened. As the FDA started approving more marijuana-based medications, the push to unify the two systems accelerated. These new FDA drugs undercut the justification for state-run medical marijuana systems, and states faced pressure from the feds to conform to a new, unified standard for all marijuana businesses. There are still vestiges of the states' medical marijuana laws that remain in 2030. In a handful of states, qualified patients can still register as medical marijuana patients. This carries benefits such as exemption from taxes on certain marijuana purchases or having purchases covered by insurance.[XXI] State-run systems are fading away, but not quickly.

[XXI]The Washington State legislature asked three agencies to come up with rules to help unify its two marijuana systems. In October of 2013, the agencies suggested changes to the state's medical marijuana law, including reducing the amount a patient could possess to only three ounces from 24 ounces and eliminating home growing. This is still higher than the one-ounce limit for other users. The agencies also recommended that patients with medical marijuana cards be exempt "from state and local retail sales taxes and use taxes."
Carpenter, Mikhail. Draft Recommendations of the Medical Marijuana Work Group. Washington State Liquor Control Board. Oct 21, 2013 https://lcb.app.box.com/draft-recommendations

Chapter 10 – Criminal Justice

Enforcing marijuana prohibition was a massively expensive drain on the country that, over the decades, racked up millions of victims. Marijuana arrests in the United States peaked in 2007, with 870,000 that year, according to the FBI Uniform Crime Report. Of those arrests, the vast majority, about 775,000, were simply for marijuana possession.[109] To put those numbers in perspective, there were significantly more people arrested for marijuana than for all murders, forcible rapes, aggravated assaults, and other violent crimes in the country put together. That year, roughly one out of every 16 arrests was just for weed. In the four decades between 1970 and 2010, there were over 21.5 million arrests for marijuana in total.[110]

While the drug war did almost nothing stop Americans from using drugs, it did succeed at turning America into a nation of prisons. The so-called war on drugs was largely responsible for nearly quadrupling incarceration rates in the

U.S. in the 40 years after it began in 1971. In 2011, Americans accounted for just under 4.5 percent of the world's population, but they represented over 20 percent of its prison population. Because of the drug war, the United States was by far the global leader in both the total number of people behind bars and the number of prisoners per capita.

Roughly 2.3 million people were in prison in the U.S. in 2011, which means roughly one out of every 100 American adults was behind bars. By comparison, no other democratic, industrialized country came anywhere close. The United States' incarceration rate was almost five times higher than that of the United Kingdom's—and the UK's incarceration rate was higher than average for Western Europe. An American was roughly 10 times more likely to be in jail than a person in Denmark, Finland, or Norway.[111]

Billions were wasted each year on arresting, prosecuting, and jailing the hundreds of thousands of people arrested for marijuana. While it is difficult to accurately assess the exact cost of all this law enforcement, some estimates placed it at around $8.7 billion just for the year 2010.[112] These estimates represented only the direct cost of enforcing prohibition—leaving out the numerous long-term social costs.

Being arrested for marijuana and labeled a criminal could impact a person's earning potential for their entire life. A drug record made it more difficult for individuals to obtain higher education or find employment. For example, being convicted of a marijuana-related crime could result in a college student losing scholarships and access to federal aid. In 1998, Congress added a provision to the Higher Education Act that eliminated federal student aid eligibility for any person with a drug conviction.

Because of this provision, over 200,000 students were initially made ineligible for federal loans, grants, and work-study programs. The provision was eventually made somewhat less burdensome in 2006 and again in 2009.[113]

Even if the charges were eventually dropped, merely being falsely arrested for a small amount of marijuana could create a huge burden for a person. In certain professions like teaching, as soon as a person was arrested, their employer was immediately notified. This would easily result in suspension or worse.

Marijuana arrests ruined lives in other ways. Some people had their children taken away by protective services for even minor marijuana violations, and a drug offense could cost people the roof over their heads. In 1988, Congress passed a law requiring public housing authorities to make any drug activity grounds for eviction. It didn't even matter if the tenant was the one who was arrested. In the 2002 Supreme Court case *HUD v. Rucker*, the court ruled that if a guest, unbeknownst to the tenant, engages in drug activities, the public housing authority has the right evict an innocent tenant. The case involved a sick 79-year-old man whose full-time housekeeper hid a crack pipe in his apartment.[114]

The tremendous burden of the war on marijuana didn't fall evenly across the American people. The vast majority of this needless suffering fell on the shoulders of minorities and the poor. The war on marijuana was built upon tactics of racial fear, and through its entire history it was enforced in a shockingly racist manner. Even though whites and blacks tended to use marijuana at similar rates in the first decade of the 21st century, African-Americans were almost four times as likely to be arrested for a marijuana violation. This racial disparity in arrests was nationwide, but in some areas African-Americans were more than 15 times as likely to be arrested for marijuana as white people.[115]

Since marijuana has been fully legalized, the number of marijuana arrests has plummeted from over 870,000 in 2007 to only a few thousand in 2030, with many of them in straight states that have yet to legalize its recreational sale.[XXII] There are still arrests for such offenses as selling to minors, regulatory violations, and marijuana tax evasion, but the number of actual marijuana arrests pales in comparison to what it once was. There are also a significant number of minor, civil violations such as smoking in public, but these only result in fines like those for a parking ticket or for littering, saving the time and expense that are put into an arrest. Most importantly, these fines don't result in a record. The money wasted on enforcing marijuana prohibition has fallen to a tiny fraction of what it once was. For the most part those law enforcement resources have been redirected to far more critical issues or freed up for other government services.

[XXII] In 2005, the Netherlands had roughly 19 marijuana-possession arrests for every 100,000 people. That was 10 times lower than the United States' rate that same year of 269 per 100,000 people. It is possible for a change in policy to cause a dramatic reduction in arrests.
Feilding, Amanda. The Global Cannabis Commission Report. The Berkley Foundation. Sep 2008.
http://www.beckleyfoundation.org/Cannabis-Commission-Report.pdf

Impact on the Black Market

Legalization effectively destroyed the black market for marijuana, just like the end of alcohol prohibition mostly obliterated a once-thriving black market for booze. The criminalization of marijuana once funneled billions to street gangs in the United States and dangerous drug cartels in Latin America, but legalization effectively kicked them out of the marijuana business. This was a real blow to criminal organizations, given that marijuana was by far the most widely used illegal drug.

Decimating this black market has also helped to reduce overall arrests by eliminating many of the crimes that sprung from prohibition. Without black market profits to fight over, there was a drop in violence, gun crimes, and money laundering. Al Capone murdered numerous rivals to control the illegal liquor business in Chicago, but after the 21st Amendment was ratified, you never saw Budweiser and Coors settle their market disputes with machine guns. Marijuana doesn't make people violent, but black market profits do.

It is impossible to know exactly how much damage marijuana legalization did to drug cartels' balance sheets—criminal organizations don't tend to publish annual earnings reports—but all indications suggest a substantial hit to their business. In 2009, the U.S. Border Patrol seized roughly 2.7 million pounds of marijuana near the U.S.-Mexico border. We can only guess at how much made it through undetected. That year, marijuana accounted for 99.5 percent of all drugs seized at the border. By comparison, with just over 10,000 pounds seized, cocaine came in at a very distant second place.[116] Different estimates concluded that somewhere between 15 percent[117] to over 60 percent[118] of all cartel drug revenue came from marijuana. While there is disagreement about the exact figure, it is likely the cartels were bringing in more than a billion dollars a year from marijuana. This illicit money propped up organizations known to have killed tens of thousands of people in Mexico. Now, almost all of that money goes instead into the heavily taxed legal marijuana industry. That money now pays for schools and public health care programs instead of criminal hit squads.

Marijuana legalization also had some marginal impact on the remaining illegal drug trades. As discussed, marijuana legalization has made it less likely that people will interact with illicit drug dealers and encounter other drugs. Without marijuana, criminal organizations needed to defray their fixed costs over a much smaller market. Building a drug tunnel under the border, for example, costs the same no matter how much material moves through it.

While marijuana legalization destroyed about 95 percent of the black market in green states, it did not completely eliminate it. After all, it's possible to find some illegal or unauthorized market for almost anything. There are small, illicit markets for alcohol, tobacco, imported cheese, and even milk. Selling unpasteurized milk in the United States is illegal, and in 2010 the FDA actually launched a sting operation to catch and arrest an Amish farmer for illegally selling raw milk across state lines.[119]

The nature of this very small black market for marijuana after legalization is totally different from what it was before. One aspect is the informal illegal transaction: Technically, it's illegal to sell or trade marijuana that a hobbyist grows at home, just like it's illegal to sell beer brewed at home. It violates tax laws and laws governing commercial licenses. A friend trading some of his excess homemade weed or beer to another friend in exchange for their used lawnmower is technically a crime, but one that is rarely if ever prosecuted.

The true illicit market for marijuana is centered on avoiding high local excise taxes on pot that has been legally produced. This is very similar to the black market for cigarettes. Mainly, it involves buying packaged marijuana in lower-tax states and driving it to higher-tax locations to sell it for profit out of the back of a truck. Going through the effort of setting up an unlicensed, large-scale growing operation to produce marijuana to sell illegally is simply not profitable. While this illegal marijuana is not subject to excise taxes, the added inefficiencies and risk make it tough to beat the legitimate market. Most people don't like dealing with criminals. They prefer the incredible convenience of legitimate stores, the better selection offered, and the guarantee of quality.

Still, this sort of tax-evasion scheme has been a problem with cigarettes for years. In 2012, states' excise taxes on a pack of cigarettes varied significantly, from as low as $0.17 a pack in Missouri to as high as $4.35 in New York state.[120] Combined with the relatively lax enforcement of anti-tobacco smuggling laws, this disparity created an opening for people willing to break the law. They could move the cigarettes across state lines, sell them at a noticeable discount, and still make a profit. The larger the local disparity in tax rates, the more prevalent tax evasion became. This same issue also exists for alcohol, but the larger size and greater weight of the product makes it far less common. The problem persists with marijuana because of the difference in local taxes, but it is a relatively small one. The federal government learned from the mistakes around cigarette smuggling at the beginning of the 21st century and actively took steps to reduce the problem with marijuana.

The federal government's efforts to prevent interstate marijuana smuggling consists of three main parts. The biggest weapon in the federal arsenal is being able to make states adopt a relatively uniform tax rate for marijuana indirectly. The smaller the disparity between marijuana taxes, the less profit there is in smuggling. This is why the federal government adopted a secondary excise tax on marijuana that is applied unless marijuana is subject to local taxes of equal or greater size. As a result, marijuana prices are fairly uniform across the country. Theoretically, it would be simpler to establish a single federal excise tax across the entire country, but the federal government doesn't have the legal authority to stop states from creating their own taxes, and senators would never have agreed to let the federal government take this lucrative source of revenue that their states had become accustomed to. Like many things in politics, the result is a needlessly complex, suboptimal compromise that is simply good enough.

The second weapon against tax evasion is the seed-to-sale tracking system. Since the beginning of legalization, marijuana was subjected to significantly more oversight than cigarettes ever were. It's incredibly difficult to divert legally produced marijuana out of the system to avoid taxes—a truckload of marijuana can't go missing without the government noticing. In addition, the strict origin labeling required on marijuana products also made it easier to investigate these cases. Using the labels, police can easily track the marijuana back to where it was produced and find out exactly when it was moved into the gray market. The government's final tool is personal possession limits.

Personal Possession Limits

Next to the register at T&R Cannabis is a small sign that says, "Purchases are limited to eight ounces of marijuana." The Durham CCC store has as similar sign, but the limit is 150 grams, or just under six ounces. In California, the limit is technically set at one pound, but unlike other states, California doesn't require retail stores to have a sign. All of these limits are far more than what any sane individual would ever need to purchase in a single shopping trip, but if they tried to buy more, they'd be turned down.

When the first states started legalizing marijuana before it was approved federally, they adopted personal possession/purchase limits. In both Washington State and Colorado, the original limit was one ounce per adult. Possessing more than that was still a crime. The limits prevented marijuana from being bought in massive quantities at licensed retail locations and then diverted into states where it was still illegal. The potential interstate commerce problem was guaranteed to attract the attention of the federal government. In 2013, the Department of Justice put out a memo stating that they would take a mostly hands-off approach in states that legalized marijuana, unless certain problems emerged, including "diversion of marijuana from states where it is legal in some form to other states."[121]

After federal legalization, this became less of a problem and the limits were significantly relaxed in many places, but the concept was left in place. Limits serve a useful function stopping systematic criminal tax evasion. The assumption is that no regular person has a legitimate reason to have more than two pounds of marijuana unless they are trying to do something illegal, like selling it without paying taxes. An excessive possession infraction is much easier to prove in court than tax evasion or selling without a license. While still on the books, these laws are normally invoked only in egregious violations. The goal is to go after real criminals, not individuals exceeding the limit by an ounce or two.

Chapter 11 – Industrial Hemp

While in 2030 you won't be driving by giant open fields of marijuana, there are many places in the country where you can see beautiful, endless fields of its close cousin growing over 10 feet high. If you are really determined, you can probably do it while wearing a hemp shirt, munching on a snack containing hemp seeds, and driving a car with hemp door panels, all of which was produced in the United States.[XXIII] There was probably no single part of America's absurd experiment with marijuana prohibition that was more ridiculous than its effective

---

[XXIII] The new BMW i3 uses hemp fibers in the door panels to reduce weight.
Reiter, Chris and Maier, Angela. BMW Electric Offered With Spare SUV to Ease Range Anxiety. Bloomberg. July 29, 2013.
http://www.bloomberg.com/news/2013-07-28/bmw-electric-offered-with-spare-suv-to-ease-range-anxiety.html

ban on industrial hemp. It was one of the many collateral casualties of the war on drugs. The federal government finally again approved industrial hemp before it legalized recreational marijuana but there is probably no way hemp would have been approved if the country hadn't started to turn against the entire idea of marijuana prohibition.

Hemp was in essence outlawed because the 1970 Controlled Substances Act made all varieties of cannabis a Schedule I drug, regardless whether it could be used as a drug or not. The law stated:

The term "marihuana" means all parts of the plant Cannabis sativa L., whether growing or not; the seeds thereof; the resin extracted from any part of such plant; and every compound, manufacture, salt, derivative, mixture, or preparation of such plant, its seeds or resin. Such term does not include the mature stalks of such plant, fiber produced from such stalks, oil or cake made from the seeds of such plant, any other compound, manufacture, salt, derivative, mixture, or preparation of such mature stalks (except the resin extracted therefrom), fiber, oil, or cake, or the sterilized seed of such plant which is incapable of germination.[122]

Technically, the Controlled Substances Act didn't prohibit the cultivation of hemp, but growing it required approval from the Drug Enforcement Administration. The problem was that the DEA refused to provide commercial licenses to grow it, making it impossible for American farmers to grow non-intoxicating industrial hemp. Despite the fact that the cannabis breed for industrial hemp produces only the tiniest trace amounts of THC, DEA Administrator Asa Hutchinson in 2001 took the ridiculous position that "many Americans do not know that hemp and marijuana are both parts of the same plant and that hemp cannot be produced without producing marijuana."[123] For a long time, the closest the DEA came to permitting the growth of hemp was in 1999, when it provided a temporary permit to the University of Hawaii to grow a small quarter-acre test plot. Even after multiple states around the turn of the 21st century passed laws to expressly approve the cultivation of industrial hemp, the DEA still refused to allow farmers to grow it.[124]

The federal government maintained the insupportable position that since hemp technically contains trace amounts of THC and is technically the same species as marijuana, it must be prohibited. When directly petitioned about hemp, the Obama administration in 2012 said, "Federal law prohibits human consumption, distribution, and possession of Schedule I controlled substances. Hemp and marijuana are part of the same species of cannabis plant. While most of the THC in cannabis plants is concentrated in the marijuana, all parts of the plant, including hemp, can contain THC, a Schedule I controlled substance."[125]

Industrial hemp and the strains of marijuana grown to be smoked are both technically members of the species Cannabis sativa—in the same way that a wild gray wolf and a pure breed Pomeranian are both technically members of the species Canis Lupus. In both cases, though, thousands of generations of selective breeding made them radically different from one another.

Industrial hemp was purposefully bred to be used for fiber and/or seeds. You can't get high off of industrial hemp. The plant contains only the most miniscule amount of THC, normally less than half a percent. It would be physically impossible to consume enough hemp to equal an active dose. The biological fact is that producing THC requires a significant energy and nutrient investment by the plant. As a breeder of industrial hemp, you want the plant to produce the maximum amount of fiber or seeds possible. The last thing you want is the plant to waste energy making THC.

Hemp was bred for fiber and food. The long stalks of the plant are a very useful, fast-growing source of fiber and biomass. The strong natural fiber is used to make paper, cordage, textiles, insulation, carpet, animal bedding, car parts, and many other products. Hemp was traditionally used to make canvas, which is why the name canvas derives from cannabis. The seeds are edible and are a highly nutritious food source, containing a surprisingly balanced combination of fats and essential amino acids. Hemp seeds are an extremely good source of omega-3. They can be consumed directly, ground into a powder, or processed into food products like hempmilk. The seeds can also be pressed for their oil, which can be used in cooking or in products such as paint, cosmetics, or fuel.

Ditchweed

Nothing illustrated what a senseless waste the United States' war on marijuana was like its fight against "ditchweed."

In the early days of the republic, hemp was a very popular agricultural product grown throughout the states. It was needed to make cordage for America's large maritime industry and to make the canvas for the iconic covered wagons of pioneers. Thanks to developments that allowed wood pulp to be used for paper and to the importation of cheap, strong fibers from Asia, America's hemp production dropped significantly in the early 1900s.

In 1942, after the Philippines fell to Japan, cutting off a big source of cordage, the United States government encouraged patriotic farmers to grow industrial hemp as part of the war effort. During the war years, hundreds of thousands of acres of American soil were planted with hemp. A byproduct of this widespread growth of agricultural hemp was that in many places the plant went feral, establishing itself in the wild. The nickname of "weed" applied to the cannabis plant is apt, given that it can grow like one. It is a hardy plant that can grow in a wide variety of climates and conditions.

Feral hemp, or "ditchweed," was thought to have no value to anyone as a drug. Like the industrial hemp it descends from, it contains only trace amounts of THC, making it useless as an intoxicant. Nevertheless, the federal government spent $175 million over two decades trying to eradicate ditchweed as part of its war on marijuana.[126]

In 2005, law enforcement in the United States proudly boasted that they had eradicated some 223 million marijuana plants. It sounds impressive, yet of that, 98 percent—roughly 219 million plants—were ditchweed. Of all the millions of plants destroyed by the government, less than 2 percent were intended to be used for marijuana.[127] While the destruction of feral hemp helped inflate statistics to make a good talking point, it did nothing to stop people from using marijuana.

The most ironic part of the story is that the government efforts to destroy feral hemp may have made it slightly easier for some people to grow clandestine marijuana outside. When trying to grow high-THC marijuana, the goal is to raise only unfertilized female plants, which produce the maximum amount of THC-rich flowers, or "buds." Fertilized female marijuana produces fewer buds and more seeds. Nearby male, feral hemp plants can potentially fertilize female marijuana plants, reducing their yield. Trying to grow a second generation of marijuana from a seed that resulted from fertilization by hemp would produce an inferior product. The government's senseless war on ditchweed is a solid metaphor for the entire war on marijuana: Huge amounts of money and resources were spent trying to achieve a goal, yet the result was counterproductive.

The Market for American Hemp

Most other countries didn't follow America's nonsensical move of outlawing a useful and completely benign crop simply because it was related to a drug. While the United States was stopping its farmers from growing hemp, it was a common farm product in other countries including Canada, China, Chile, France, Russia, Spain, etc.

It wasn't until states started legalizing marijuana that the political stigma in Congress surrounding anything marijuana-related waned sufficiently enough that Americans could grow industrial hemp again. The first serious attempt to legalize hemp in Congress was in 2013, after two states had already fully legalized marijuana. The House approved an amendment to the farm bill allowing industrial hemp to be grown for research purposes, but the overall measure failed for unrelated reasons.[128] Restrictions on growing hemp were removed largely in parallel with those on marijuana. The more comfortable with marijuana Americans got, the more absurd the ban on hemp became.

While allowing the growth of hemp in the United States has increased overall demand slightly, it remains a niche product in 2030. For decades while Americans were prohibited from growing hemp, they could still import it, and there was an established world market. Back in 2011, when hemp was still illegal in the United States but allowed in most of the world, the annual harvest was 52,000 tons of hemp fiber. By comparison, there were 227,000 tons of flax fiber and tow and 26,000,000 tons of cotton lint produced.[129] While hemp is versatile, it was not destined to be a miracle plant that could revolutionize American farming. Today, it remains one of many useful crops available to American farmers.

While the amount of domestic industrial hemp produced is modest, its economic benefit for American farmers extends beyond the value of each year's crop. Hemp is a very hardy plant that requires little in the way of herbicide or pesticide. Its fast-growing nature tends to suppress any weeds. It is also very disease-resistant. A 1998 white paper in North Dakota found that hemp would be easier on the soil than most other crops that can grow in the state, concluding that "basically, industrial hemp is easier on the land than any other crops except for legumes such as clover and alfalfa."[130] Accordingly, hemp makes for a good rotational crop. Merely having the option of growing hemp gives farmers greater flexibility in adjusting to market and weather conditions.

Chapter 12 – How and Why It Happened

Now that you've seen what marijuana legalization might look like in 2030, I have decided to break with this narrative for the rest of the book. I want to travel back in time to the present, in order to consider our path from the current situation to my vision of the future. I know I'm predicting some rapid change, but all indicators show rapid change is coming. I want explain why we can reasonably expect that in less than a decade, the federal government will end its prohibition against marijuana.

Large cultural shifts do not arise because laws are amended. Rather, as public opinion changes, the politics around an issue change. For the most part, politicians in a democracy are not really leaders, they are followers. Even though it doesn't always work out in practice, the whole point of a democracy is that politicians' actions should reflect the will of the electorate.

Probably the single biggest factor in the inevitability of marijuana legalization in the near future is demographics. Even though nothing significant involving marijuana happened that year, 1950 marks a watershed moment for marijuana reform. People born before 1950 likely never tried marijuana when they were young, nor knew friends who did. For the most part, they continued never to touch the stuff as they got older. With little direct experience with marijuana, this generation was far more likely to believe the "reefer madness" style propaganda and consider its use immoral. They are still more likely to believe that marijuana is inherently a "gateway drug," and they are the generation most skeptical that marijuana has any medical benefits. Accordingly, as polling consistently shows, this generation is by far the most opposed to marijuana policy reform. In 2013, Pew Research found that a large majority of adults under the age of 65 think marijuana should be legal, but only 33 percent of senior citizens support legalization. The poll found that 64 percent of young adults (age 18-29) support legalization, as do 53 percent of Americans near retirement (age 50-64).[131] The divide between young and middle-aged Americans is much smaller than that between senior citizens and people only a decade or two younger.

Americans born after 1950 tend to have had a completely different personal experience with cannabis. They likely tried marijuana when they were young or at least knew many people who did. They doubted many of the government's anti-marijuana claims—or even outright laughed at them. Adults who have tried marijuana are significantly more likely to support legalization. The data shows how sharp this generational divide really is. A 1967 Gallup survey of college students found that only five percent of students had tried marijuana. By 1971, that figure had jumped to 51 percent.[132] Other polling from the time shows this trend was not limited to colleges, but was widespread among all young Americans. Starting around 1970, there was a veritable explosion of marijuana use among young Americans, and it has remained popular ever since.

The older generation of prohibitionists, to put it bluntly, is dying off, and dead people don't often vote. In 2010, there were around 28 million Americans born before 1950, making up roughly 12 percent of the United States population.[133] Yet by 2020, about half the people in this group are expected to have passed on. They will go from a major voting bloc to only a minor segment of the electorate. The same goes for lawmakers. Currently 169 out of the 535 members of Congress were born before 1950, but only 37 were born before 1940.[134] This generation, with its antiquated thinking about marijuana, will quickly start disappearing from the halls of Congress and will be replaced by a new generation.

Even if no one changed their minds about marijuana legalization, support for it will grow at a solid pace thanks to natural population replacement, but there are also powerful social forces pushing the country toward greater acceptance of marijuana. Opinions about marijuana and its legal status have been shifting dramatically even within each generation. In just the past 18 years, support for marijuana legalization has essentially doubled among Baby Boomers, Generation Xers, and the Silent Generation. When combined with demographic changes, social trends are powering a dramatic political change.

The Unwinnable War

Among the factors driving this cultural shift, a major one is that the war on marijuana now seems unwinnable and not worth the effort to most Americans. The war on drugs as a whole has resulted in millions of arrests, billions spent on enforcement, and the funneling of massive amounts of money to criminal organizations. It has been instrumental in the explosion in the prison population, which, in addition to its social harms, has stressed state budgets. From 1980 to 2011, the share of California's General Fund that went toward corrections increased by 436 percent. In 2011, the state was spending more on locking people up than on higher education.[135]

And yet, all this spending has produced no net gains. There are almost no metrics you can point to that don't make the war on marijuana look like an abject failure. As of 2012, marijuana usage rates were on par with those from 1971, when President Richard Nixon launched his war on drugs. Despite waging a "war" to stop people from smoking pot, the marijuana peddled by the black market has gotten cheaper and noticeably stronger for the past several decades.[136]

Most Americans have now gotten the message about the failure of the war on drugs, which has made them more open to the case for legalization. The Pew Research poll from 2013 found that 72 percent of Americans believe the government efforts to enforce marijuana laws cost more than they are worth. Similarly, a Rasmussen poll from the same year found 82 percent believe the United States is not winning the war on drugs.[137]

The Role of the Internet

The Internet has ensured that this information is readily available to the American public. The failings of prohibition, which for a time could be easily ignored by the media and politicians, are continuously pushed to the forefront of conversation in the digital arena. The role the Internet is playing in advancing the cause of marijuana legalization simply can't be understated.

Unlike past generations that relied on getting their information from just a few mainstream media sources, the Internet generation has access to literally hundreds of news sources—many of them more open-minded about marijuana or even openly supportive of it. Back in the 1980s, if one sought a pro-marijuana legalization news source, one had to actually go out and buy one of a limited number of specialty magazines like High Times. The Internet completely changed this. Anyone, anywhere, at any time can now access a whole range of news sources, studies, and opinions about marijuana. Finally, much of this information is outside the direct control of the government or big news networks.

As a society, we no longer depend on a top-down trust structure in our news: There is now a massive peer-to-peer trust structure as well. With tools like Facebook, email, and Twitter, a piece of information or a story from a small news outlet can go viral. Few subjects in the early Internet era were more viral than marijuana reform. The peer-to-peer dynamic has made it easy to refute the government's misinformation—the propaganda just couldn't hold up against the new flood of information.

The Internet has also become the primary medium through which to organize marijuana-reform activism. The rapid spread of the Internet significantly changed politics at every level, but it was especially powerful for the issue of marijuana reform. Given that marijuana legalization is a youth-driven issue and that young people were the first to embrace new Internet trends, there has been a natural fusion. When the marijuana legalization initiative Proposition 19 was on the ballot in California in 2010, it had the largest Facebook page of any political campaign in the state—dramatically more than those of the top candidates for the governor's office or the U.S. Senate.

With the online amplification of the call for marijuana reform, it became an issue that politicians were forced to confront. The fact that regular people keep pushing the issue on almost every online forum makes it hard for politicians and the media to ignore. President Obama exploited the Internet as an organizing tool to drive his 2008 campaign, but once in office, he was repeatedly forced to answer regular Americans' questions about marijuana legalization because of the Internet. With just about every attempt the Obama administration made to connect with voters through online forums that allowed people to vote on a topic, the conversation was overwhelmingly driven back to the subject of legalization and drug policy reform. The top-voted question in Obama's 2009 digital town hall was about legalizing marijuana.[138] When in January of 2011 Obama had a YouTube question-and-answer session, 99 of the top 100 questions were about marijuana or drug policy reform.[139] Later that same year, when the Obama administration created an online petition site where a question would be addressed if it had sufficient support, the first petition to reach the threshold asked, "Isn't it time to legalize and regulate marijuana in a manner similar to alcohol? If not, please explain why you feel that the continued criminalization of cannabis will achieve the results in the future that it has never achieved in the past?"[140] In 2012, when Obama did a Google Plus "hangout," not surprisingly 18 of the top 20 questions were about marijuana and drug policy reform. In his first term, Obama would normally jokingly dismiss these questions, but after the success of the marijuana initiatives in Colorado and Washington State, his administration started to take the issue more seriously.

Acceptance Breeds More Acceptance

Support for ideas doesn't often grow linearly; it frequently snowballs. The more people who support a cause, the more comfortable others feel coming forward with their own support. We see this in the growing push for marijuana legalization. Support for marijuana legalization in Pew Research's polling grew from 31 percent in 2000 to 41 percent in 2010—roughly one point a year. In just the past three years, support has grown to 52 percent. That is a roughly a three-point increase each year, and this trend appears likely to continue.

The more people experience something, the less scary it becomes. The world did not fall apart when states legalized medical marijuana back in the 1990s. These earlier reforms did not turn states into wastelands overrun by "potheads." Even in states whose lax prescription rules enabled de facto legalization, consequences have been minor. The problems that have arisen are manageable ones, certainly nothing that merits continuing an incredibly expensive and failed "war."

The presence of a regulated medical marijuana retail system in Colorado proved marijuana could be regulated and taxed by the state without causing major problems. It gave people a chance to really see what legal marijuana would be like. Many Americans' response has been, "This is not so bad." It is no surprise that given Colorado's history with medical marijuana, it became one of the first states where voters fully legalized it.

The growth of medical marijuana has also given some in older generations a positive firsthand experience with the drug. Many seniors who long opposed marijuana have turned to it for medical reasons and have come to realize it is not as bad as they once were led to believe. People once highly opposed to marijuana became more accepting when they saw how helpful and safe it was as a medicine for their sibling, spouse, or parent.

As support for marijuana legalization grows, it lessens the stigma associated with both using marijuana and supporting reform. The more economists, celebrities, news figures, and politicians say they're in favor of marijuana reform, the easier it becomes for the next individual to publicly endorse the idea. We are already seeing marijuana legalization seriously discussed in a way it never was 10 years ago. Being the first politician to endorse a controversial idea can be incredibly hard. Being the fourth politician to back a proposal can still be risky, but much easier. Being the 400th politician to support an idea will practically go unnoticed.

We recently saw this same dynamic play out with politicians' support for same-sex marriage, an issue whose public polling over the last 20 years has almost perfectly mirrored that of marijuana legalization. Back in 2004, Republicans used their anti-same-sex marriage views as a political weapon against Democrats. In 2008, supporting same-sex marriage was still considered a political risk. Almost no major politicians were behind the idea, including Barack Obama, who opposed it in his 2008 presidential campaign. At the time, only eight sitting senators had endorsed same-sex marriage. By early 2011, the number of sitting senators in support of marriage equality had grown only to 15, but the issue would soon reach a tipping point, and support soon started growing exponentially. By May of 2012, President Obama announced he had changed his mind and now supported marriage equality, and by April of 2013, a majority of senators backed the idea.[141] In just nine years, support for marriage equality went from unthinkable to the dominant political opinion in the Senate. Marijuana polling is seeing the same rapid growth in public support.

The Path to Legalization

Before reviewing how marijuana is most likely to be legalized, it's worth looking back at the end of alcohol prohibition.

If you ask when alcohol prohibition ended, the most common answer is December 5, 1933—the day Utah became the 36th state to ratify the 21st Amendment, which repealed the 18th Amendment. This is the only time in America's history an amendment was repealed by another amendment.

While this is technically a correct answer—if I were a contestant on "Jeopardy!" this is probably the answer I'd go with—in reality, the process was far more complicated and gradual. Prohibition didn't disappear overnight; it was a policy that was rolled back over decades.

One could easily argue that prohibition effectively ended eight months earlier on April 7, 1933, when the Cullen-Harrison Act went into effect. It was after signing this law that Franklin D. Roosevelt quipped, "I think this would be a good time for a beer." The act legalized the sale of beer with an alcohol content of 3.2 percent by weight, which is the equivalent of 4 percent by volume.[XXIV]

On that day, Americans all over the country gathered at bars, taverns, and breweries to enjoy their first legal drink of beer in over a decade. It was this moment, more than the ratification of the 21st Amendment, that has been memorialized with iconic photos of people "celebrating the end of prohibition" with a tall glass of beer.

But in important ways, alcohol prohibition began to end even earlier. It became clear to large majorities of America well before 1933 that the "noble experiment" with prohibition had failed, and states started taking legal action to bring it to an end. For example, in 1930 Massachusetts voters overwhelmingly approved an initiative repealing the state's "baby Volstead Act," which enforced prohibition at the state level. Voters determined that their state government would no longer enforce prohibition, leaving the task completely up to the federal government. This was a remarkable turnaround in public opinion, given that only six years earlier, in 1924, a referendum to repeal the state's prohibition failed to win approval in the state.[142]

During the next election cycle, voters in several states, including Colorado, California, and Washington, followed suit and approved statewide initiatives repealing their own state-based prohibition laws. The success of these ballot measures helped signal the death knell for prohibition. They made

---

[XXIV] The Cullen-Harrison Act redefined "intoxicating liquors," as were prohibited under the 18th Amendment, as beverages that contained more than 3.2 percent alcohol by weight. Previously, the limit was set at 0.5 percent.

enforcement even more difficult and sent a clear message to Congress that the American people no longer supported prohibition. Multiple states had stopped enforcing prohibition laws by the time the 21st Amendment was finally ratified. It is impossible to ignore the parallels with what voters in Colorado and Washington State decided regarding marijuana in 2012.

Alternatively, it is possible to make the case that alcohol prohibition in the United States didn't end in 1933, but ended much later. The 21st Amendment didn't make alcohol legal across the United States—it simply gave each state the choice to set its own policy regarding prohibition. The amendment reads:

> **Section 1.** The eighteenth article of amendment to the Constitution of the United States is hereby repealed.

> **Section 2.** The transportation or importation into any State, Territory, or possession of the United States for delivery or use therein of intoxicating liquors, in violation of the laws thereof, is hereby prohibited.

> **Section 3.** This article shall be inoperative unless it shall have been ratified as an amendment to the Constitution by conventions in the several States, as provided in the Constitution, within seven years from the date of the submission hereof to the States by the Congress.

The second section was designed to give states the option of remaining dry, and for several years many states chose to do just that. It wasn't until 1966 that Mississippi finally became the last state to end prohibition. Yet even after that, Mississippi, like many other states, adopted local option rules allowing individual counties or towns to remain dry. Well into the 21st century, large sections of the country prohibit alcohol sales.

Alcohol prohibition in the United States didn't begin or end in a day. It was a policy that took decades for the country to reverse, first at the state level and then at the federal level and then again at the state level, with several small and large legal actions along the way. It could even be argued, given the sheer number of dry counties, that the process of ending alcohol prohibition is still incomplete.

All indicators suggest that marijuana legalization will take a similar path. Already, states have started using the ballot initiative process to legalize marijuana in defiance of federal marijuana laws. The American people overwhelmingly prefer a 21st Amendment-style solution that would leave marijuana's legal status entirely up to individual states. A CBS News poll taken soon after the 2012 election found 59 percent of Americans think state governments should decide whether or not marijuana is legal, while only 34 percent think the federal government should make this decision.[143] Similarly, a Gallup poll from the same time found 64 percent of Americans don't want the federal government trying to enforce the federal marijuana prohibition in states that have legalized the drug.[144] This proposal has broad bipartisan support. Conservatives tend to oppose marijuana legalization but consider the states' rights aspect more important. Liberals also back it because they tend to support marijuana legalization and see it as the fastest way to make it a reality.

Marijuana Legalization, from the States to the Federal Level

The importance of the ballot initiative process to marijuana reform simply can't be overstated.

In 1996, California became the first state to approve medical marijuana when 56 percent of voters approved Proposition 215. A total of seven states and the District of Columbia voted to approve the use of medical marijuana via ballot measures before it was finally approved via a state legislature, as it was in Hawaii in 2000.[145] Medical marijuana spread quickly to more liberal states with ballot initiative laws, but much more slowly in states without it. Without the ballot initiative, legalization in this country could have easily been delayed for another 20 to 30 years.

Direct democracy was a key goal of progressive reformers around the end of the 19th century. It was seen as a way to get around an often corrupt system in which the two parties refused to change a status quo they each benefited from. This push by progressives for direct democracy came when many western territories were drafting their first state constitutions and gaining statehood. As a result, the ballot initiative laws are far more common west of the Mississippi.

The ballot initiative—the process by which regular citizens can put a proposal on the ballot and the entire electorate can directly choose to accept or reject it—has proven to be one of the most important forms of direct democracy. It allows people to deal with issues that have broad popularity but which, for reasons stemming from partisan advantage, political corruption, or powerful interest groups, elected representatives have refused to address.

For example, the ballot initiative was key in establishing both the direct election of United States senators and presidential primaries. Prior to the 17th Amendment, senators were selected by state legislatures. State legislators were reluctant to give up this power, and members of the U.S. Senate didn't have much interest in amending the Constitution to change the system that got them elected in the first place. In 1908, voters in Oregon used the initiative process to enact a law giving voters the power to directly elect their two senators. The passage of this initiative began a nationwide wave. In the next election cycle, Oregon again used the initiative process to create the first presidential primary, starting another national trend and putting the selection of a party's presidential nominee in the hands of regular voters instead of party bosses.[146]

While every other amendment to the Constitution approved by Congress was ratified by state legislatures, the 21st Amendment is unique in that it operated like a ballot measure—it was ratified by state conventions specially created solely for a vote on the proposed amendment. This amendment process has only ever been used once, and it was because supporters of the 21st Amendment feared temperance groups with powerful lobbying operations that had outsized influence over local politicians. Here's how it works: Regular citizens register to run as "opposed" or "in favor" delegates. Then, an election is held in which people vote either for "opposed" delegates or "in favor" delegates. The delegation that receives the most votes then goes to the convention, where they vote up or down on the proposed amendment. While this by-proxy procedure is technically not direct democracy, it has the same effect.

Given marijuana policy reform's broad popular support and the fact that it has remained weirdly taboo among politicians, the ballot initiative is crucial. In 2013, 52 percent of the country supported marijuana legalization, but only 17 members of the House of Representatives—that is, only 3.9 percent of the chamber—sponsored HR 499, the Ending Federal Marijuana Prohibition Act of 2013.[147] This imbalance is a real problem.

Part of the imbalance is due to the generational divide. At the beginning of 2013, the average age of a member of the House of Representatives was 58; in the Senate, the average age was 61.[148] Clearly, Congress is much older than the adult population as a whole. The people in power are disproportionately from a generation whose thoughts about marijuana are well outside the mainstream. It's natural to expect that the imbalance in the perception of marijuana reform between the populace and its representatives will correct itself as an older generation, less amenable to reform, retires from government service.

Polling shows that liberals tend to be the most supportive of marijuana legalization, while conservatives are less supportive, so legalization should spread to the liberal states first. It is also likely that legalization will spread first via ballot measure. Only after voters in half a dozen states adopt legalization can we expect the tide to begin to shift, with more state legislatures finally feeling comfortable adopting their own legalization laws.

Step by Step

2012 - The process of marijuana legalization really began with the 2012 election. That year, legalization ballot measures in

Colorado and Washington State succeeded, but an underfunded and badly written initiative in Oregon failed. This election sent two clear messages: that a well drafted initiative with a solid campaign was needed for victory, and that the American people are ready to look seriously at ending our failed war on marijuana.

Legalization in Washington and Colorado had broad national and international consequences. It gives other countries a justification to withdraw or ignore international treaties against marijuana legalization, including the Single Convention on Narcotic Drugs of 1961. To the extent that these treaties have any real force, it is due to the United States' lead in the international war on marijuana. With America now unable to stop its own states from legalizing marijuana, the federal government has lost its moral authority as well as its ability to push other countries around on this issue. It is no coincidence that Uruguay moved forward with its plan to legalize marijuana—a plan that closely mirrors the new law in Colorado—only a few months after the 2012 election. If Colorado and Washington State are the laboratories that propel legalization forward in the United States, then Uruguay may play a similar role in Latin America. There is already growing talk among many Latin American leaders about the failure of the drug war and the need for new approaches.

2014 – The next state to legalize marijuana will likely be Alaska. At the time of this book's publication, there is a well-funded campaign working to put a legalization initiative on Alaska's 2014 primary ballot. Alaska has several factors going for it. The most important is that Alaska has the youngest population in the country—only 8.1 percent of the population is over age 65, compared to a national average of 13.3 percent. The state also has a strong libertarian streak.

One or two other states may put initiatives on the 2014 general election ballot, but not many are likely to. At the time of publication, Oregon is the one other state with a real shot. For now, marijuana reform groups are primarily focused on 2016, since it is a presidential election. Strong youth turnout is important for the success of legalization initiatives, and voter participation among young adults is much lower in non-presidential elections. Most estimates assume that the turnout difference alone between an off-year election and a presidential year election would cost a marijuana legalization ballot initiative about two points of support.

2016 – This is the year the tidal wave is going to hit. If current polling trends hold, national support for marijuana legalization should rise to well over 60 percent by 2016. Marijuana reform groups are already planning to take advantage of this presidential election year to make their big push. There are likely to be ballot initiatives in Arizona, California, Maine, Massachusetts, and Nevada. If a well-crafted initiative makes the ballot in these states, they are almost guaranteed to pass. As of 2013, local polls showed there is already majority support for legalization in all five of these states, and support should continue to grow over the next three years.

Of these states, I suspect the biggest impact of legalizing marijuana will come in Massachusetts. California, Colorado, Washington, and Nevada all have relatively self-contained metro areas—relatively few people commute daily across their borders.

Massachusetts, on the other hand, borders five other states, all of which have significant populations close to the Massachusetts state line. In about 30 minutes, you can drive from Manchester, N.H.; Providence, R.I.; Hartford, CT; Bennington, VT; or Albany, N.Y., to the Massachusetts border. The majority of people in New Hampshire and Rhode Island live less than an hour from the state. Legalizing marijuana in Massachusetts would make it foolish for the rest of New England to keep it illegal. All these other states have already decriminalized possession, so the real question they will face is whether they'll let the tax revenue flow to Massachusetts just to maintain an unpopular prohibition that has clearly failed.

With marijuana legalization on so many ballots during a presidential election year, including the potentially important swing state of Nevada, the major-party candidates will be forced to address the issue. I don't expect a major presidential candidate to fully endorse legalization that year, but the politics of the situation will likely force them to publicly favor a hands-off approach by federal agencies. Neither party can risk pissing off young voters, and promising to leave states alone is very popular with both the Democratic and Republican base. This is the kind of half-solution, designed to try to please everyone without directly committing to anything, that politicians in tough elections are drawn to like moths to a flame.

2017 –This is when the fight is likely to move from the ballot to the state legislature. After voters in multiple states approve legalization, politicians in other states will feel comfortable backing the idea—or political pressure will force them to approve it. It's very likely that Vermont, Hawaii, and

Rhode Island will move forward with marijuana legalization in early 2017 or 2018. They are three of the most liberal states in the country and have a history of being progressive on marijuana reform: Hawaii was the first state legislature to adopt medical marijuana, Vermont was the second, and Rhode Island was the third. I also expect the changing political environment created by a wave of victories in 2016 to push many state legislatures to adopt smaller reforms, such as reducing their penalties for simple possession.

At the same time, several foreign countries will probably adopt legalization. The political situation in Canada regarding this issue is worth watching, because it could put some real pressure on the United States to finally act. In 2013, the leader of the Liberal party of Canada endorsed marijuana legalization,[149] and there is a very good chance his party could win back control after the next federal election likely to take place at the end of 2015. If the Liberals are serious about moving forward with marijuana reform, a smart time to do it would be right after the United States' 2016 election, when several American states on or near the Canadian border are likely to legalize marijuana.

2018 – Most targets that allow ballot initiatives will probably have been hit in 2016, so the 2018 election is unlikely to be a big year at the ballot. There will probably be one or two initiatives in states like Michigan or Montana, and a few more state legislatures will move forward with legalization.

2020 – By the time of the 2020 presidential election, I suspect roughly a quarter of the country will have legalized marijuana, and popular support for legalization could easily be over 65 percent if current trends hold. Federal politicians will be forced to discuss the egregious federal/state conflict in marijuana laws and how it should be addressed. It is easy to envision how activists could use this election to really push the federal government to adopt a solution by strategically placing initiatives on the ballot in Ohio and Washington, D.C. No one has won the White House since 1960 without carrying Ohio. As a crucial swing state, it normally gets the bulk of presidential campaign stops and spending. Placing legalization on the 2020 Ohio ballot would make the issue unavoidable for the presidential candidates.

Having an initiative legalizing the retail sale of marijuana in Washington, D.C., would leave members of Congress with no choice but to address it. D.C. is the most liberal standalone jurisdiction in the country, and polling from early 2013 shows there is already majority support for legalization. The holdup is that the district's local laws are subject to review by Congress. In 1998, the residents of D.C. overwhelmingly voted for a medical marijuana initiative, but Congress stepped in and stopped the city from implementing the law for over a decade.[150] This review process is a serious problem for residents of D.C., but it can be exploited by activists to send a message. If the people of D.C. approve full legalization in the 2020 election, members of Congress will have only two options. They can either step in to stop the law—sure to be a very unpopular move by that time— or they can allow the law to go into effect in the nation's capital, which, with public marijuana stores just blocks from Department of Justice, will highlight how impractical the federal law against marijuana will have become.

These factors, combined with the natural turnover in Congress, should create the political space to change the federal law regarding marijuana in the congressional term of 2021-2022. Given the American public's overwhelming preference for marijuana's legal status to be left up to the states, a federal legalization bill that allows for that is the most likely outcome. You can rarely count on Congress to choose the best solution, but you can safely bet on them choosing the politically easiest option. The federal law legalizing marijuana will probably echo the 21st Amendment, because it will likely be the product of the same basic political compromises.

Once this federal issue is finally resolved, that should open the floodgates. I suspect at least a dozen state legislatures will legalize marijuana a year or two later, but not all of them. It is reasonable to assume that some conservative states will be very slow to fully embrace marijuana legalization. Yet even these conservative states won't be immune to the changing political climate and the reality of marijuana being commercially sold in nearby states. I suspect they will remove or dramatically reduce their penalties for marijuana possession. Eventually, I think all states will likely succumb to the pressure and fully legalize marijuana, but that might not be for several decades after the federal law is changed.

Conclusion

This book is intended to provide what I consider to be a very likely outcome for marijuana legalization, while also laying out the range of possibilities. One of the big slogans for the marijuana reform movement right now is "regulate it like alcohol," but in a huge, diverse country with a long history of complex alcohol laws, that can mean many things.

My hope is to get people thinking about the most significant regulatory issues, but by no means is this overview complete. Volumes could, and probably will be, written by the thousands of different federal, state, and local government agencies that will have some say over the legal rules for marijuana. My goal was not just to list what the regulatory issues will be, but also to indicate what political and economic forces are most likely to shape them. I want people to understand who the relevant players will likely be, where the minor legal fights should take place, and what political dynamics will drive the debate. In this way, one can anticipate which leverage points will shape the future.

If you are really interested in or concerned about legalization, do not ask, 'What will legal marijuana be like?' but rather, 'What do I want legal marijuana to be like?' Despite criminalization's numerous problems, victims, and failings, it has the benefit of being conceptually very simple. It is a blunt policy ax: marijuana is simply illegal. The only real questions are how much effort to put into enforcement and how harshly to punish violations. Legalization, on the other hand, offers a dizzying spectrum of interlocking choices. If given free rein to rewrite every law in the country, you could make marijuana only legal for a few heavily licensed non-profit growing co-ops, or you could set the rules so almost anyone could order a side of joints at every fast food drive-thru in the country.

Legally and practically, there is very little restricting what the government could choose to do with legal marijuana, and thanks to decades of practical experience regulating alcohol and tobacco, we have a very good idea of just how to shape the rules to get outcomes we want. Using the basic tools of regulation and taxation, the government could direct the legal market for marijuana almost any way it sees fit. The government could make marijuana incredibly cheap by exempting it from all taxes and allotting it farm subsidies, or it could make it very expensive by applying huge excise taxes. It could ensure the industry is dominated by only a handful of companies by strictly limiting the number of production licenses it provides, or it could force the market to be extremely diverse by putting hard caps on ownership. Taxes could be structured to favor low-quality weed or high-quality bud. The entire system could be run directly as a government monopoly, as a regulated private sector, or as a hybrid of the two. Marijuana could be allowed to be sold at every grocery store, gas station, and market in the country. Or it could be limited to just a tiny number of specially regulated retailers, government-run stores, or only pharmacies like the current proposal in Uruguay.

What I personally find so exciting about this moment is that, as a society, we are presented with a blank canvas. This is an incredible, unique situation in which we have a chance to design a major industry from the ground up—and we've got a very good idea of how to do it. We currently have a huge range of options to choose from that will affect every aspect of how people buy, use, and even think about marijuana. We can make the legal marijuana market into almost anything we want. The decisions we are currently making and will make in the near future will likely shape the issue for the next century, if not longer. This is not just boring regulation, this is social engineering on a large scale.

This amazing window of opportunity, though, will likely be open only for the next decade. Once any system gets rolling, inertia quickly takes over. People develop habits, interest groups form, the industry creates powerful lobbying operations, and stakeholders will fight to maintain the new status quo. If you want to make a serious impact on the future, now is the time.

About the Author

Jon Walker is a senior policy analyst for Firedoglake.com, where in 2009 he helped guide the progressive conversation regarding health care reform. In 2010, he helped launch FDL's Just Say Now campaign to support marijuana legalization efforts across the country. He is a graduate of Wesleyan University.

Notes

[1] Swift, Art. For First Time, Americans Favor Legalizing Marijuana. Gallup Oct 22, 2013.
http://www.gallup.com/poll/165539/first-time-americans-favor-legalizing-marijuana.aspx

[2]Clinton Tried Marijuana as Student, He Says. New York Times, March 30, 1992.
http://www.nytimes.com/1992/03/30/news/30iht-bill_1.html

[3] Anslinger, H.F. and Cooper, Courtney Ryley. Marijuana – Assassin of Youth. The Reader's Digest. Feb 1938.
http://www.druglibrary.org/schaffer/history/e1930/mjassassinrd.htm

[4] Walker, Jon. Prop 19 Opponents Terrified by Centuries-Old Tradition of Local Ordinances. Firedoglake. Sep 17, 2010.

http://elections.firedoglake.com/2010/09/27/prop-19-opponents-terrified-by-centuries-old-tradition-of-local-ordinances/

[5] Editorial Board. Snuff Out Pot Measure. Los Angeles Times. Sep 24, 2010.
http://articles.latimes.com/2010/sep/24/opinion/la-ed-prop19-20100924

[6] Meyer, Jeremy P. When pot smells in Denver, the Nasal Ranger goes in to investigate. Denver Post. Nov 11, 2013.
http://www.denverpost.com/politics/ci_24496810/when-pot-smells-denver-nasal-ranger-goes-investigate

[7] Alonso, Martin Barriuso. Cannabis Social Clubs in Spain. Series on Legislative Reform of Drug Policies. Jan 2011.
http://www.tni.org/sites/www.tni.org/files/download/dlr9.pdf

[8] Visit section. Jack Daniels website.
http://www.jackdaniels.com/visit

[9] Burkhart, Jeff. The Great Experiment, Prohibition Continues. National Geographic assignment blog. Aug 19, 2010.
http://ngablog.com/2010/08/19/the-great-experiment-prohibition-continues/

[10] Ingold, John. Colorado marijuana stores likely to be concentrated in few cities. Denver Post. July 25, 2013.
http://www.denverpost.com/ci_23733574/colorado-marijuana-stores-likely-be-concentrated-few-cities

[11] Stutz, Howard. Maryland vote dismays casino operator Penn National. Las Vegas Review-Journal. Nov 7, 2012.
http://www.reviewjournal.com/business/casinos-gaming/maryland-vote-dismays-casino-operator-penn-national

[12] About Us. Vermont Department of Liquor Retail Website. http://802spirits.com/about_us

[13] Kumar, Anita and Helderman, Rosalind. McDonnell is handed legislative defeat as Virginia assembly drops bill to privatize liquor stores. Washington Post. Feb 9, 2011. http://www.washingtonpost.com/wp-dyn/content/article/2011/02/08/AR2011020806203.html

[14] Maynard, Melissa. Should States Get Out of the Booze Business? Stateline. April 4, 2013. http://www.pewstates.org/projects/stateline/headlines/should-states-get-out-of-the-booze-business-85899465064

[15] Banse, Tom. Liquor Privatization In Washington State, One Year Later. OPB. May 30, 2013. http://www.opb.org/news/article/npr-liquor-privatization-in-washington-state-one-year-later/

[16] General election results 2010. California Secretary of State. http://www.sos.ca.gov/elections/sov/2010-general/maps/prop-19.htm

[17] Permanent Rules Related to the Colorado Retail Marijuana Code. Colorado Department of Revenue. Sep 9, 2013. http://www.colorado.gov/cs/Satellite/Rev-MMJ/CBON/1251592984795

[18] Candy and Fruit Flavored Cigarettes Now Illegal in United States; Step is First Under New Tobacco Law. FDA News Release. Sep 22, 2009. http://www.fda.gov/NewsEvents/Newsroom/PressAnnouncements/ucm183211.htm

[19] A little History. Four Roses website.

http://www.fourrosesbourbon.com/a-little-history/

[20] Scherer, Michael. What Is President Obama's Problem With Medical Marijuana? Time. May 3, 2012. http://swampland.time.com/2012/05/03/what-is-president-obamas-problem-with-medical-marijuana/#ixzz1tqDDjgiQ

[21] Wenner, Jann S. Ready for the Fight: Rolling Stone Interview with Barack Obama. Rolling Stones. April 25. 2012. http://www.rollingstone.com/politics/news/ready-for-the-fight-rolling-stone-interview-with-barack-obama-20120425?page=2

[22] Leff, Lisa. Harborside Health Center, Oakland Pot Shop, Hit With $24 Million Tax Bill. Huffington Post. Oct 4, 2011. http://www.huffingtonpost.com/2011/10/04/harborside-health-center-tax-bill_n_995139.html

[23] Kim, Victoria and Romney, Lee. Feds raid home of Oaksterdam University founder Richard Lee. Los Angeles Times Blog. April 2, 2012. http://latimesblogs.latimes.com/lanow/2012/04/richard-lee-home-raided.html

[24] Olson, Dan. Honeycrisp apple losing its patent protection, but not its appeal. Minnesota Public Radio. Oct 21, 2007. http://minnesota.publicradio.org/display/web/2007/10/11/honeycrisp

[25] Raustiala, Kal and Sprigman, Chris. Can Marijuana "Brands" Be Legally Protected Against Copying? Freakonomics. Aug 22, 2012. http://freakonomics.com/2012/08/22/can-marijuana-%E2%80%9Cbrands%E2%80%9D-be-legally-protected-against-copying/

[26] Initiative 502 Adopted Rules. Washington State Liquor Control Board. Oct 16, 2013.
http://lcb.wa.gov/marijuana/initiative_502_proposed_rules
[27] History of American Beer Timeline. Beeradvocate.
http://beeradvocate.com/beer/101/history_american_beer
[28] FDA Warning Letters issued to four makers of caffeinated alcohol beverages. FDA News Release. Nov. 17, 2010.
http://www.fda.gov/NewsEvents/Newsroom/PressAnnounceme nts/ucm234109.htm
[29] What is the Cost? The Federal War on Patients. Americans for Safe Access. June 2013
http://american-safe-access.s3.amazonaws.com/documents/WhatsTheCost.pdf
[30] Hargreaves, Steve. Marijuana dealers get slammed by taxes. CNN Money. Feb 25, 2013
http://money.cnn.com/2013/02/25/smallbusiness/marijuana-tax/index.html
[31] Update on Application Process for Registered Marijuana Dispensaries. Massachusetts Health and Human Services. Oct 4, 2013.
http://www.mass.gov/eohhs/gov/departments/dph/programs/hc q/medical-marijuana/registered-marijuana-dispensary-application-process.html
[32] Presentation to Ways and Means Subcommittee on Transportation and Economic Development. Oregon Liquor Control Commission. March 20, 2013
https://olis.leg.state.or.us/liz/2013R1/Downloads/CommitteeM eetingDocument/9001

[33] Tax Policy. Distilled Spirits Council of the United States.
http://www.discus.org/policy/taxes/

[34] Illicit Tobacco. United States Government Accountability Office. March 2011.
http://www.gao.gov/assets/320/316372.pdf

[35] WHO Report on the Global Tobacco Epidemic, 2013, Enforcing bans on tobaccos advertising, promotion, and sponsorship. World Health Organization. 2013.
http://www.who.int/tobacco/global_report/2013/en/index.html

[36] Television ads. New Approach Washington.
http://www.newapproachwa.org/page/television-ads

[37] Okrent, Daniel. Wayne B. Wheeler: The Man Who Turned Off the Taps. Smithsonian Magazine. May 2010.
http://www.smithsonianmag.com/history-archaeology/Wayne-B-Wheeler-The-Man-Who-Turned-Off-the-Taps.html

[38] Scranton, Philip. The Great Beer Parade Stimulus of 1932. Bloomberg. May 21, 2012.
http://www.bloomberg.com/news/2012-05-21/the-great-beer-parade-stimulus-of-1932.html

[39] Cooper, Michael. Struggling Cities Turn to a Crop for Cash. New York Times. Feb 11, 2012.
http://www.nytimes.com/2012/02/12/us/cities-turn-to-a-crop-for-cash-medical-marijuana.html?_r=0

[40] Grim, Ryan. California Pot Initiative Opposed By Beer Industry. Huffington Post. Sep 21, 2010.
http://www.huffingtonpost.com/2010/09/21/this-buds-not-for-you-bee_n_732901.html

[41] Boonn, Ann. State Cigarette Excise Tax Rates and Rankings. Campaign for Tobacco-free Kids. Aug 1, 2012. http://www.tobaccofreekids.org/research/factsheets/pdf/0097.pdf

[42] Smoking and Tobacco Use Fact Sheet. Centers for Disease Control and Prevention. http://www.cdc.gov/tobacco/data_statistics/fact_sheets/fast_facts/

[43] Saad, Lydia. In U.S., 38% Have Tried Marijuana, Little Changed Since '80s. Gallup. Aug 2, 2013. http://www.gallup.com/poll/163835/tried-marijuana-little-changed-80s.aspx

[44] Endorsements. Yes on Prop AA website. http://www.yesonpropaa.com/endorsements/

[45] Newport, Frank. Record-High 50% of Americans Favor Legalizing Marijuana Use. Gallup. Oct 17, 2011. http://www.gallup.com/poll/150149/record-high-americans-favor-legalizing-marijuana.aspx

[46] House Clerk Roll Call Vote on Children's Health Insurance Program Reauthorization Act of 2009. Jan 14, 2009. http://clerk.house.gov/evs/2009/roll016.xml

[47] Seitz-Wald, Alex. Grover Norquist Gives Thumbs Up to Pot Taxes. National Journal. Oct 24, 2013. http://www.nationaljournal.com/congress/grover-norquist-gives-thumbs-up-to-pot-taxes-20131024

[48] Tax and Fee Rate. Alcohol and Tobacco Tax and Trade Bureau. http://www.ttb.gov/tax_audit/atftaxes.shtml

[49] Lottery Sales and Transfers. North American Association of State and Provincial Lotteries. 2013.
http://www.naspl.org/index.cfm?fuseaction=content&menuid=17&pageid=1025

[50] Underwood, Madison. ABC agents raid Birmingham beer and wine store, take homebrewing equipment. AL.com Blog. Sep 20, 2012.
http://blog.al.com/spotnews/2012/09/abc_agents_raid_birmingham_bee.html

[51] Chappell, Bill. Home Brewing: Soon to Be Legal in All 50 States. NPR. May 8, 2013
http://www.npr.org/blogs/thetwo-way/2013/05/08/182317722/homebrewing-soon-to-be-legal-in-all-50-states

[52] Legal statute reference page. American Homebrewers Association.
http://www.homebrewersassociation.org/pages/government-affairs/statutes/united-states

[53] Stiffler, Christopher. Amendment 64 would produce $60 million in new revenue and savings for Colorado. Colorado Center on Law and Policy. Aug 12, 2012.
http://www.cclponline.org/postfiles/amendment_64_analysis_final.pdf

[54] Trautmann, Franz Kilmer, Beau and Turnbull, Paul. Further Insights into aspects of the EU illicit drug market. European Commission. 2013.
http://ec.europa.eu/justice/anti-drugs/files/eu_market_summary_en.pdf

[55] Newport, Frank. U.S. Drinking Rates Edges Up Slightly to 25-Year High. Gallup. July 30, 2010
http://www.gallup.com/poll/141656/drinking-rate-edges-slightly-year-high.aspx
[56] Cone, EJ Johnson, RE Darwin, WD Yousefnejad, D Mell, LD Paul, BD and Mitchell, J. Passive inhalation of marijuana smoke: urinalysis and room air level of delta-9-tetrahydrocannabinol. Journal of Analytical Toxicology. May-June 1987.
http://www.ncbi.nlm.nih.gov/pubmed/3037193
[57] Terpeluk, Paul. Opposing view: Why we won't hire smokers. USA Today. Jan 29, 2012.
http://usatoday30.usatoday.com/news/opinion/story/2012-01-29/Cleveland-Clinic-not-hiring-smokers/52873896/1
[58] Phung, An. Cops Handing Out Doritos Instead of Tickets at This Year's Hempfest. NBC Bay Area. Aug 15, 2013.
http://www.nbcbayarea.com/news/national-international/Cops-Handing-Out-Doritos-Instead-of-Tickets-at-This-Years-Hempfest-219808091.html
[59] Open Containers in Public. Open Containers Laws.com.
http://www.opencontainerlaws.com/opencontainersinpublic.html
[60] Code of Iowa Sec 123.46
http://coolice.legis.iowa.gov/cool-ice/default.asp?category=billinfo&service=iowacode&ga=83&input=123.46
[61] LaMance, Ken. Open Container Laws by State. LegalMatch. March 18, 2010.

http://www.legalmatch.com/law-library/article/open-container-laws-by-state.html

[62] Understanding California's new Smokefree Housing Law. Center for Tobacco Policy and Organizing. Nov 2011. http://www.hcd.ca.gov/codes/rt/Understanding%20California%27s%20New%20Smokefree%20Housing%20Law.pdf

[63] St. John, Sarah. 40 years ago: Kansas AG raids Amtrak train, confiscates liquor. Lawrence Journal-World. July 19, 2012. http://www2.ljworld.com/news/2012/jul/19/40-years-ago-kansas-ag-raids-amtrak-train-confisca/

[64] A Brief Review of Alcoholic Beverages in Kansas. Kansas Wine & Spirits Wholesalers Association. http://kwswa.org/history

[65] Roche, Lisa Riley. Utah's private clubs fade into history Wednesday. Deseret News. June 30, 2009. http://www.deseretnews.com/article/705313829/Utahs-private-clubs-fade-into-history-Wednesday.html?pg=all

[66] Sewell, R. Andrew Poling, James and Sofuoglu, Mehmet. The effects of cannabis compared with alcohol on driving. American Journal on Addiction. May-June 2009. http://www.ncbi.nlm.nih.gov/pmc/articles/PMC2722956/

[67] White, Joseph B. Nissan Expects to Market Self-Driving Cars by 2020. Wall Street Journal. Aug 27, 2013. http://online.wsj.com/article/SB10001424127887323407104579038832031956964.html

[68] Sewell, R. Andrew Poling, James and Sofuoglu, Mehmet. The effects of cannabis compared with alcohol on driving. American Journal on Addiction. May-June 2009.

http://www.ncbi.nlm.nih.gov/pmc/articles/PMC2722956/

[69] Marijuana Vaporizer Provides Same Level of THC, Fewer Toxins Study Shows. Science Daily. May 16, 2007. http://www.sciencedaily.com/releases/2007/05/070515151145.htm

[70] Park, Alice, Goodbye, Big Soda: New York Becomes First City to Ban Large-Sized Soft Drinks. Time. Sep 13, 2012. http://healthland.time.com/2012/09/13/goodbye-big-soda-new-york-becomes-first-city-to-ban-large-sized-soft-drinks/

[71] Kilmer, Beau Caulkins, Jonathan P. Pacula, Rosalie Liccardo MacCoun, Robert J. and Reuter, Peter H. Altered State? Assessing How Marijuana Legalization Could Influence Marijuana Consumption and Public Budgets. RAND. 2010. http://www.rand.org/content/dam/rand/pubs/occasional_papers/2010/RAND_OP315.pdf

[72] Miron, Jeffery A. and Zwiebel, Jeffery. Alcohol Consumption During Prohibition. The American Economic Review. May 1991. http://www.nber.org/papers/w3675

[73] Results from the 2012 National Survey of Drug Use and Health. Substance Abuse and Mental Health Services Administration. Sep 2013. http://www.samhsa.gov/data/NSDUH/2012SummNatFindDetTables/DetTabs/NSDUH-DetTabsSect1peTabs1to46-2012.htm#Tab1.1A

[74] Majority Now Supports Legalizing Marijuana. Pew Research. April 4, 2013.

http://www.people-press.org/2013/04/04/majority-now-supports-legalizing-marijuana/

[75] Donnelly, N. Hall, W. D. and Christie, P. The effects of partial decriminalisation on cannabis use in South Australia, 1985 to 1993. Australian Journal of Public Health. 1995. http://espace.library.uq.edu.au/view/UQ:153257

[76] Drug Policy in Connecticut and Strategy Options. Connecticut Law Revision Commission. Jan 21, 1997. http://www.cga.ct.gov/lrc/drugpolicy/drugpolicyrpt2.htm#SecDZ

[77] Harper, Sam Stumpf, Erin C. and Kaufman, Jay S. Do Medical Marijuana Laws Increase Marijuana Use? Replication Study and Extension. Annals of Epidemiology. March 2012. http://www.annalsofepidemiology.org/article/S1047-2797%2811%2900372-3/abstract

[78] World Drug Report 2013. United Nations Office of Drug and Crime. 2013. http://www.unodc.org/wdr/

[79] 2011 Annual report on the state of the drugs problem in Europe. European Monitoring Centre for Drugs and Drug Addiction. November 2011. http://www.emcdda.europa.eu/publications/annual-report/2011

[80] Trends in Current Cigarette Smoking Among High School Students and Adults, United States, 1965-2011. Centers for Disease Control and Prevention. Dec 7, 2012. http://www.cdc.gov/tobacco/data_statistics/tables/trends/cig_smoking/index.htm

[81] National Survey of American Attitudes on Substance Abuse XVII: Teens. The National Center on Addiction and Substance Abuse at Columbia University. Aug 2012.
http://www.casacolumbia.org/upload/2012/20120822teensurvey.pdf

[82] Anderson, D. Mark Hansen, Benjamin and Ress, Daniel I. Medical Marijuana Laws and Teen marijuana Use. IZA. May 2012.
http://ftp.iza.org/dp6592.pdf

[83] Malick, Amy. Study: Pot Increase Heart Attack Risks. ABC News. June 2012
http://abcnews.go.com/Health/story?id=117399&page=1

[84] Whan, Lynne B. West Mhairi C. L. McClure, Neil. And Lewis, Sheena E. M. Effect of delta-9-tetrahydrocannabinol, the primary psychoactive cannabinoid in marijuana, on human sperm function in vitro. Fertility and Sterility. March 2006.
http://www.fertstert.org/article/S0015-0282%2805%2903942-7/abstract

[85] Tetrault, Jeanette M. Crothers, Kristina Moore, Brent A. Mehra, Reena Concato, John and Fiellin, David A. Effects of Marijuana Smoking on Pulmonary Function and Respiratory Complications. JAMA Internal Medicine. Feb 2007.
http://archinte.jamanetwork.com/article.aspx?articleid=411692

[86] Hashibe, MiaMorgenstern, Hal Cui, Yan Tashkin, Donald P. Zhang, Zuo-Feng Cozen, Wendy Mack, Thomas M. and Greenland, Sander. Marijuana Use and the Risk of Lung and Upper Aerodigestive Tract Cancers: Results of a Population-

Based Case-Control Study. Cancer Epidemiology, Biomarker & Prevention. Oct 2006
http://cebp.aacrjournals.org/content/15/10/1829.full
[87] Arkowitz, Hal and Lilienfeld Scott O. Experts Tell the Truth about Pot. Scientific American. Feb 22, 2012.
http://www.scientificamerican.com/article.cfm?id=the-truth-about-pot
[88] Gmel, Gerhard Kuendig, Hervé Rehm, Jürgen Schreyer, Nicolas and Daeppen, Jean-Bernard. Alcohol and cannabis use as risk factors for injury – a case-crossover analysis in a Swiss hospital emergency department. BMC Public Health. Jan 2009.
http://www.biomedcentral.com/1471-2458/9/40
[89] Reiss, Albert J. and Roth Jeffery A. Understanding and Preventing Violence, Volume 3: Social Influences. National Academies Press. 1994.
http://www.nap.edu/openbook.php?record_id=4421&page=40 3
[90] Deaths from Marijuana v. 17 FDA-Approved Drugs. Procon.org. July 8, 2009.
http://medicalmarijuana.procon.org/view.resource.php?resource ID=000145
[91] Vital Signs: Overdoses of Prescription Opioid Pain Relievers — United States, 1999—2008. Centers for Disease Control and Prevention. Nov 1, 2011.
http://www.cdc.gov/mmwr/preview/mmwrhtml/mm6043a4.htm

[92] Blum, Deborah. The Chemist's War. Slate. Feb 19, 2010. http://www.slate.com/articles/health_and_science/medical_exa miner/2010/02/the_chemists_war.html

[93] Lead Poisoning Due to Adulterated Marijuana. The New England Journal of Medicine. April 10, 2008. http://www.nejm.org/doi/full/10.1056/NEJMc0707784

[94] Randerson, James. Warning issued over cannabis adulterated with glass beads. The Guardian. Jan 12, 2007. http://www.theguardian.com/society/2007/jan/12/drugsandalco hol.drugs

[95] Hecht, Peter. Lab helps medical marijuana growers self-regulate product safety. McClatchy. April 5, 2010. http://www.mcclatchydc.com/2010/04/05/91596/lab-helps-medical-marijuana-growers.html

[96] Hamadeh R, Ardehali A, Locksley RM, and York MK. Fatal aspergillosis associated with smoking contaminated marijuana, in a marrow transplant recipient. American College of Chest Physicians. Aug 1988. http://www.ncbi.nlm.nih.gov/pubmed/3293934,

[97] Marijuana Linked to Salmonellosis. New York Times. May 27, 1987. http://www.nytimes.com/1982/05/27/us/marijuana-linked-to-salmonellosis.html

[98] Wilson, Jacque. 3 deaths may be tied to synthetic marijuana in Colorado. CNN. Sep 7, 2013. http://edition.cnn.com/2013/09/06/health/synthetic-marijuana-denver/

[99] Trautmann, Franz Kilmer, Beau and Turnbull, Paul. Further Insights into aspects of the EU illicit drug market. European Commission. 2013.
http://ec.europa.eu/justice/anti-drugs/files/eu_market_summary_en.pdf

[100] Mack, Alison and Joy, Janet. Marijuana As Medicine? National Academies Press. 2000.
http://www.nap.edu/openbook.php?record_id=9586&page=14

[101] Naftali T, Bar-Lev Schleider L, Dotan I, Lansky EP, Sklerovsky Benjaminov F, and Konikoff FM Cannabis induces a clinical response in patients with Crohn's disease: a prospective placebo-controlled study. Clinical Gastroenterology and Hepatology. May 4, 2013.
http://www.ncbi.nlm.nih.gov/pubmed/23648372#

[102] Ware, Mark. Etc. Smoked cannabis for chronic neuropathic pain: a randomized controlled trial. Canadian Medical Association Journal. Aug 30, 2010.
http://www.cmaj.ca/content/182/14/E694.abstract

[103] Lakhan, Shaheen and Rowland, Marie. Whole plant cannabis extracts in the treatment of spasticity in multiple sclerosis: a systematic review. BMC Neurology. 2009.
http://www.biomedcentral.com/1471-2377/9/59

[104] Guidance for Industry Complementary and Alternative Medicine Products and Their Regulation by the Food and Drug Administration. U.S. Food and Drug Administration. Updated March 2, 2007
http://www.fda.gov/RegulatoryInformation/Guidances/ucm144657.htm

[105] Warning Letter to General Mills, Inc. U.S. Food and Drug Administration. May 5, 2009 http://www.fda.gov/iceci/enforcementactions/warningletters/ucm162943.htm

[106] FDA approves first anti-diarrheal drug for HIV/AIDS patients. U.S. Food and Drug Administration. Dec 31, 2012. http://www.fda.gov/NewsEvents/Newsroom/PressAnnouncements/ucm333701.htm?source=govdelivery

[107] Vastag, Brian. Marijuana study of traumatized veterans stuck in regulatory limbo. Washington Post Oct 1, 2011. http://articles.washingtonpost.com/2011-10-01/national/35279253_1_marijuana-study-marijuana-for-clinical-research-government-grown-marijuana

[108] Frequently asked questions about Medical Marijuana (Cannabis) in Washington State. Washington State Department of Health. http://www.doh.wa.gov/YouandYourFamily/IllnessandDisease/MedicalMarijuanaCannabis/GeneralFrequentlyAskedQuestions.aspx

[109] Uniform Crime Reports 2007. Federal Bureau of Investigation. Sep 2008. http://www.fbi.gov/about-us/cjis/ucr/crime-in-the-u.s/2007

[110] Belville, Russ. NORML's Big Book of Marijuana Facts. NORML. http://stash.norml.org/bigbook/arrests-by-admin.html

[111] Walmsey, Roy. World Prison Population List (Ninth Edition). International Centre for Prison Studies. July 2011.

http://www.prisonstudies.org/publications/list/179-world-prison-population-list-9th-edition.html

[112] Miron, Jeffery A. and Waldock, Katherine. The Budgetary Impact of Ending Drug Prohibition. CATO Institute. Sep 2010.
http://www.cato.org/publications/white-paper/budgetary-impact-ending-drug-prohibition

[113] The Higher Education Act. Students for Sensible Drug Policy.
http://ssdp.org/campaigns/the-higher-education-act/

[114] Nieves, Evelyn. Drug Ruling Worries Some in Public Housing. New York Times. Mar 28, 2002.
http://www.nytimes.com/2002/03/28/us/drug-ruling-worries-some-in-public-housing.html?src=pm

[115] The War on Marijuana in Black and White. American Civil Liberties Union. June 2013.
https://www.aclu.org/criminal-law-reform/war-marijuana-black-and-white-report

[116] US-Mexico border drug seizures App. Center for Investigative Reporting. http://static.apps.cironline.org/border-seizures/

[117] Kilmer, Beau, Caulkins, Jonathan P. Bond, Brittany M. and Reuter, Peter H. Reducing Drug Trafficking Revenues and Violence in Mexico. RAND. 2010.
http://www.rand.org/content/dam/rand/pubs/occasional_papers/2010/RAND_OP325.pdf

[118] Fainaru, Steve and Booth, William. Cartels Face and Economic Battle. Washington Post. Oct 7, 2009. http://www.washingtonpost.com/wp-dyn/content/article/2009/10/06/AR2009100603847.html

[119] Eng, James. Amish farmer targeted by FDA raids shuts down raw milk business. U.S. News on NBCnews.com Feb 15, 2012. http://usnews.nbcnews.com/_news/2012/02/15/10418406-amish-farmer-targeted-by-fda-raids-shuts-down-raw-milk-business?lite

[120] State Excise Tax Rates on Cigarettes. Federation of Tax Administrators. Jan 2013. http://www.taxadmin.org/fta/rate/cigarette.pdf

[121] Justice Department Announces Update to Marijuana Enforcement Policy. U.S. Department of Justice. Aug 29, 2013. http://www.justice.gov/opa/pr/2013/August/13-opa-974.html

[122] Controlled Substance Act. U.S. Food and Drug Administration. http://www.fda.gov/regulatoryinformation/legislation/ucm1487 26.htm

[123] DEA Clarifies Status of Hemp in the Federal Register. Drug Enforcement Agency. Oct 9, 2001. http://www.justice.gov/dea/pubs/pressrel/pr100901.html

[124] Johnson, Renee. Hemp as an Agricultural Commodity. Congressional Research Service. July 24, 2013. http://www.fas.org/sgp/crs/misc/RL32725.pdf

[125] Kerlikowske, Gil. What We Have to Say About Marijuana and Hemp Production. We the People White House.

https://petitions.whitehouse.gov/response/what-we-have-say-about-marijuana-and-hemp-production

[126] Smith, Phillip. Hemp: DEA Has Spent $175 Million Eradicating "Ditch Weed" Plants That Don't Get You High. Stop the Drug War. Jan 4, 2007. http://stopthedrugwar.org/chronicle/2007/jan/04/hemp_dea_has_spent_175_million_e

[127] 98 Percent of All Domestically Eradicated Marijuana Is "Ditchweed," DEA Admits. NORML. Sep 7, 2006. http://norml.org/news/2006/09/07/98-percent-of-all-domestically-eradicated-marijuana-is-ditchweed-dea-admits

[128] Grim, Ryan. Bipartisan Hemp Amendment Passes House Over DEA Objections. Huffington Post. June 6, 2013. http://www.huffingtonpost.com/2013/06/20/hemp-amendment_n_3472967.html

[129] Production. Food and Agriculture Organization of the United Nations. http://faostat3.fao.org/faostat-gateway/go/to/download/Q/*/E

[130] Kraenzel, David G. Pety, Tim, Nelson, Bill Anderson, Marshall J. Mathern, Dustin Todd, Robert. Industrial Hemp as an Alternative Crop in North Dakota. July 23, 1998. http://ageconsearch.umn.edu/handle/23264

[131] Majority Now Supports Legalizing Marijuana. Pew Research. April 4, 2013. http://www.people-press.org/2013/04/04/majority-now-supports-legalizing-marijuana/

[132] Harrison, Lana D., Michael Backenheimer and James A. Inciardi. Cannabis use in the United States: Implications for policy. Centrum voor Drugsonderzoek. 1995.
http://www.cedro-uva.org/lib/harrison.cannabis.03.html

[133] Werner, Carrie A. The Older Population: 2010. United States Census Bureau. Nov 2011.
http://www.census.gov/prod/cen2010/briefs/c2010br-09.pdf

[134] List of current United State Senators by age. Wikipedia.org.
http://en.wikipedia.org/wiki/List_of_current_United_States_Se nators_by_age
List of current members of the United States House of Representatives by age. Wikipedia.org.
http://en.wikipedia.org/wiki/List_of_current_members_of_the_ United_States_House_of_Representatives_by_age

[135] Anand, Prerna. Winners and Losers: Corrections and Higher Education in California. California Common Sense. Sep 5, 2012.
http://www.cacs.org/ca/article/44

[136] Werb, Dan Kerr, Thomas Nosyk, Bohdan Steffanie, Strathdee Motaner, Julio and Wood, Evan. The temporal relationship between drug supply indicators: an audit of international government surveillance systems. BMJ Open. 2013.
http://bmjopen.bmj.com/content/3/9/e003077.full.pdf+html

[137] 82% Say U.S. Not Winning War on Drugs. Rasmussen Reports. Aug 18, 2013.
http://www.rasmussenreports.com/public_content/politics/gene

ral politics/august 2013/82 say u s not winning war on dr ugs

[138] Stolberg, Sheryl Gay. Obama's twist on town hall; top Internet query was about marijuana. Seattle Times. March 27, 2009. http://seattletimes.com/html/politics/2008932586 obama27.ht ml

[139] Grim, Ryan. Obama Barraged By Pot Questions For Upcoming YouTube Town Hall. Huffington Post. Jan 27, 2011. http://www.huffingtonpost.com/2011/01/27/obama-youtube-pot-questions n 814811.html

[140] Sasso, Brendan. Petition to legalize pot is first to hit White House threshold; ET proposal close. The Hill. Sep 22, 2011. http://thehill.com/blogs/hillicon-valley/technology/183411-marijuana-legalization-first-online-petition-to-require-white-house-response

[141] Matthews, Dylan. In 2011, only 15 senators backed same-sex marriage. Now 49 do. UPDATE: Now 51! Washington Post. April 2, 2013. http://www.washingtonpost.com/blogs/wonkblog/wp/2013/04/02/in-2011-only-15-senators-backed-same-sex-marriage-now-49-do/

[142] Statewide Ballot Questions —Statistics by Year: 1919 – 2012. Secretary of the Commonwealth of Massachusetts. http://www.sec.state.ma.us/ele/elebalm/balmresults.html#year1 930

[143] Backus, Fred and Condon, Stephanie. Poll: Nearly half support legalization of marijuana. CBS News. Nov 29, 2012. http://www.cbsnews.com/8301-250_162-57556286/poll-nearly-half-support-legalization-of-marijuana/

[144] Newport, Frank. Americans Want Federal Gov't Out of State Marijuana Laws. Gallup. Dec 10, 2012. http://www.gallup.com/poll/159152/americans-federal-gov-state-marijuana-laws.aspx

[145] Hawaii Becomes First State to Approve Medical Marijuana Bill. New York Times. June 15, 2000. http://www.nytimes.com/2000/06/15/us/hawaii-becomes-first-state-to-approve-medical-marijuana-bill.html

[146] Oregon. Initiative & Referendum Institute at the University of Southern California. http://www.iandrinstitute.org/Oregon.htm

[147] Govtrack.us. H.R. 499: Ending Federal Marijuana Prohibition Act of 2013. https://www.govtrack.us/congress/bills/113/hr499

[148] Fink, Jessica. Meet the New Congress: Facts and Figures About the 113th. PBS News Hour. Jan 3, 2013. http://www.pbs.org/newshour/rundown/2013/01/meet-the-new-congress-facts-and-figures-about-the-113th.html

[149] Justin Trudeau wants to legalize marijuana in order to 'keep it out of the hands of our kids'. National Post. July 24, 2013. http://news.nationalpost.com/2013/07/24/justin-trudeau-wants-to-legalize-marijuana-in-order-to-keep-it-out-of-the-hands-of-our-kids/

[150] Hohmann, James and Craig, Tim. Vote moves D.C. closer to medical marijuana. Washington Post. Dec 14, 2009. http://articles.washingtonpost.com/2009-12-14/news/36919758_1_medical-marijuana-marijuana-policy-project-hyde-amendment

44806186R00112

Made in the USA
Lexington, KY
09 September 2015